FAMILY & FRIENDS

FACILITATOR'S GUIDE

Helping the Person You Care About in Recovery

Dale W. McCleskey

LifeWay Press
Nashville, Tennessee

ACKNOWLEDGEMENTS

Family and Friends: Helping the Person You Care About in Recovery Facilitator's Guide
Copyright ©1995 LifeWay Press

LifeWay Press books are published by The Sunday School Board, 127 Ninth Avenue, North, Nashville, Tennessee 37234

For help for facilitators and leaders in carrying out LIFE® Support Group Series ministries in your church, call 1-615-251-5613.

Item 7200-24
ISBN 0-8054-9871-0
Dewey Decimal Number 306.85
Subject Heading: FAMILY LIFE/COUNSELING

Unless otherwise indicated, biblical quotations are from the *New American Standard Bible* (NASB) © The Lockman Foundation, 1960, 1962, 1963, 1968, 1971, 1972, 1973, 1975, 1977. Used by permission.

Printed in the United States of America

Contents

Covenant 5

Introduction 6

Purpose: Why *Family and Friends*? 8

Facilitator Qualifications 10

Steps for Starting a Group 14

How to Succeed as a Leader 20

Support or Discovery Group? 23

Opportunities and Challenges 24

Optional Introductory Session: Preparation for Unit 1 26

Group Session 1: Support Group Life 28

Group Session 2: Recovery as a Journey 31

Group Session 3: Impact of a Dysfunctional Family 34

Group Session 4: Bonding and Boundaries 37

Group Session 5: Shame and Identity 39

Group Session 6: Looking to the Future 41

Group Session 7: Anger 43

Group Session 8: Addiction 46

Group Session 9: Depression 50

Handouts for Group Sessions 53

Sample promotional letters 58

Feelings Poster 61

Promotion Ideas 62

Church Study Course 63

About the Author

Dale McCleskey is editor of LIFE® Support Group Series materials at the Baptist Sunday School Board. He was a pastor for 15 years before joining the Sunday School Board.

Family and Friends: Helping the Person You Care About in Recovery Facilitator's Guide
Debbie Colclough, Editor

LIFE® Support Group Series Editorial Team
Betty Hassler, Design Editor
Dale McCleskey, Editor
Kenny Adams, Manuscript Assistant

David Walley, Team Leader/LIFE® Support Group Series Specialist

Graphics by Lori Putnam
Cover Design by Edward Crawford

Family and Friends Group
COVENANT

To encourage a high level of trust, love, and openness in my *Family and Friends* group, I, _____, covenant with my group's other members to do the following.

- I agree to make attendance at all group meetings a top priority for the period for which the group meets. During these weeks I will choose this group first when making decisions about my priorities and my time. If I must be absent, I will contact my group facilitator.

- I will commit my time each week to complete the appropriate unit of study in *Family and Friends* before the group session.

- I agree to be on time for each meeting. I recognize that I hurt myself and other group members when I am late.

- I agree to stay until each meeting is adjourned. I recognize that I affect the dynamics of the group in a negative way if I leave early. My desire to leave early may be an expression of my unwillingness to face up to the feelings I am feeling in response to what is happening in the group. If I must leave the meeting early, I will explain my reasons to the group before I leave. I will be open to discussing my early departure at the next group meeting.

- I agree that what takes place in the group is CONFIDENTIAL. If I break my commitment to confidentiality, I understand that I will be asked to leave the group.

- I agree to do everything I can to help create an atmosphere of trust in the group.

- I will be patient with other group members as we allow God to work in each of our lives. I will not try to give advice or to pressure other group members to do what I think best.

- I will inform my group leader of any physical or emotional problems that might arise through my participation in the group.

- I agree to be supportive of other group members as they struggle with their emotions. When needed I will encourage other group members with the words, "I support you."

- I agree to engage in rigorous—not brutal—honesty toward myself and other group members.

- I agree to let other group members confront me in love so that I can grow.

Signed: _____ Date: _____

Group members

Introduction

Note: Page numbers identified in this facilitator's guide will be preceded by FG. All other page references refer to pages in the member's book.

More than 15 million Americans participate in some type of support group each week. An estimated 50,000 or more groups exist in the United States. The number of persons coping with such critical life issues as divorce, chemical dependency, codependency, abuse, eating disorders, low self-esteem, and dysfunctional-family matters is escalating at a phenomenal rate.

LIFE® Support Group Series materials are designed to reach out to persons who find themselves facing one or more of these emotional issues. LIFE® Support Group Series materials offer the support of a Christ-centered small-group process to bring healing and recovery in an individual's life.

Family and Friends: Helping the Person You Care About in Recovery offers this type of hope. LIFE® Support Group Series publishes these and other resources out of a commitment to the ministry Jesus offered hurting people when He said: "The Spirit of the Lord is on me, because he has anointed me to preach good news to the poor. He has sent me to proclaim freedom for the prisoners and recovery of sight for the blind, to release the oppressed, to proclaim the year of the Lord's favor" (Luke 4:18-19, NIV).

What is the LIFE® Support Group Series?

The LIFE® Support Group Series is an educational system of discovery-group and support-group resources providing Christian ministry and emotional support to individuals in areas of social, emotional, and physical need.

The *discovery group* studies resources on dysfunctional-family issues and other problem areas individuals face. A *group leader* guides group discussion of the content individuals in the group study and helps group members consider applications to their lives.

Members of discovery groups will explore personal issues and emotions, but the primary focus of the group is discussing the content in the member's book. These discovery groups generally are less emotionally intense. A caring, sensitive group leader without specialized skills or training can lead them. Because discovery groups are less intense, they provide excellent starting points for churches launching support-group ministries.

A Unique, Dual-Purpose Resource

Family and Friends: Helping the Person You Care About in Recovery is a support-group resource, but it can be used in a discovery-group format. When the leader of an effective small group ministry first examined the field-test version of *Family and Friends*, he remarked: "This is just what I have been looking for. I will use this material to acquaint the people in our church with support-group ministry." He intends to use *Family and Friends* as a discovery group for anyone interested in learning more about the support-group process. On FG page 23 you can read more about the decision to use *Family and Friends* as either a support or discovery group.

A *support group* is more specialized than a discovery group and is composed of people who meet because of personal issues common to group members. A support group focuses on helping members gain awareness; understanding; and emotional, psychological, and spiritual support for dealing with personal-life issues. While a discovery group meets to learn about a painful life issue, a support group is a group of people who all share the life issue. Support groups meet not so much to learn about but to change the pattern of thoughts, feelings, and behaviors.

Family and Friends is primarily a support group. It is written to help those who have a spouse, friend, or family member who is experiencing recovery. Because the recovery process involves major life change, it creates stresses for those who are in relationship with the recovering person. *Family and Friends* will help those individuals to understand and better relate to these changes.

LIFE® Support Group Series resources provide help for three types of support groups.

1. Encouragement and Accountability Support Group. Members encourage and support each other's progress toward a goal. A discovery-group level of leadership skills is sufficient for this type of support group. *Quitting for Good: A Christ-Centered Approach to Nicotine Dependency* is a resource example for this type of support group.

2. Personal-Issues Support Group. Members share personal responses to issues and problems with which they are dealing. The group provides a safe and loving environment for personal and spiritual healing, growth, and recovery. *Making Peace with Your Past* and *Moving Beyond Your Past* are examples of resources for this type of support group; they deal with family-of-origin issues. *Shelter from the Storm: Hope for Survivors of Sexual Abuse* is a personal-issues support group for survivors of sexual abuse. All of these groups need a skilled lay facilitator to guide the group process.

Family and Friends is a personal-issues support group. However, due to the nature of the group, *Family and Friends* does not require the level of skills necessary for the previously mentioned personal-issues groups. Personal-issues groups such as *Family and Friends; A Time for Healing: Coming to Terms with Your Divorce;* and a group for blending families require less skills of the facilitator because these groups do not deal with the complex childhood-related issues that members encounter in a group like *Making Peace with Your Past*. You will find a more extensive explanation of facilitator qualifications on FG pages 10-13. Note that one extremely important result of *Family and Friends* and the other less intense groups can be that members discover their own need to deal with childhood issues. In those cases the facilitator or leader can encourage members to participate in other support groups as appropriate.

3. 12-Step Support Group. Members use a Christ-centered adaptation of the 12 Steps to help each other make progress in recovery from addictions. The process includes repentance, trust in God, and spiritual renewal. Twelve-Step support groups also require a skilled lay facilitator to guide the group sessions.

Resources for Christ-centered 12-Step support groups include *Conquering Codependency: A Christ-Centered 12-Step Process; Conquering Eating Disorders: A Christ-Centered 12-Step Process; Conquering Chemical Dependency: A Christ-Centered 12-Step Process;* and *Conquering Chemical Dependency: First Steps to a Christ-Centered 12-Step Process.*

Purpose: Why *Family and Friends?*

People who have heard of *Family and Friends: Helping the Person You Care About in Recovery* usually scratch their heads and ask a simple question—"Why?"

Those of us who have worked to create this resource have a single—if somewhat extended—answer to the question. The single answer results in several goals for the material and for the group. The answer is this. Millions of people are working through a process of life change referred to as *recovery*. Many of those people are Christians who testify that the recovery process has helped them to experience the love and grace of God and to overcome life-destroying problems.

Unfortunately, an unwelcome side-effect often accompanies recovery. Recovery means behavior change. It can also mean an extended period of grief-work. Those who live with or care about the recovering person often have difficulty with both the grieving and the changed behavior of the person in recovery. Watching someone we care about go through an extended period of grief is uncomfortable. Having someone change routines on which we base our life stability is threatening.

Recovery can and even sometimes does result in broken relationships, alienation, and divorce. The purpose of *Family and Friends* is to help the non-recovering spouse, relative, or friend to understand and relate better to the changes the person in recovery is experiencing so that relationships may be enhanced rather than strained or broken.

Dale & Cheryl's Story

I started the recovery journey in 1986 when I began to realize that the experiences of my childhood were continuing to have a negative effect on my life as an adult. I began to participate in a support group and to work to apply to my life what I learned. From my perspective the next 18 to 24 months were a tremendously liberating, healing time of growth. However, my wife Cheryl saw things differently.

One day, after more than a year of my recovery journey, Cheryl said to me, "This is helping you, isn't it?"

At the time I had no idea what "this" she was talking about. Since I was learning better communication skills, I stopped what I was doing and asked, "What is helping me?"

She replied, "All this recovery stuff."

My immediate thought was, *Helping? My goodness, I feel like I have come alive from the dead! I feel like I have lived my life only seeing black and white, and now I see in color.* But I was learning to communicate, which is mostly listening. So I asked, "What do you mean?"

Cheryl said, "For a long time I thought all this recovery stuff was making you worse."

That conversation reflects the tension in many relationships. You see, Cheryl could only look on from the outside to see what was happening with me. The things that she saw gave a distorted picture of the recovery I was experiencing. Because of what she saw, she was concerned about the following issues.

- Cheryl saw me weeping for the first time in our 15-year marriage—and sometimes grieving deeply. This frightened her.
- Cheryl saw me developing close bonds of intimacy with people—bonds of intimacy that were based on the experiences my friends in recovery shared but that she could not understand. She feared that I might be leaving her emotionally for them.
(Note that this fear can become a destructive reality. Members in groups can develop unhealthy and destructive relationships built on the euphoria of feeling understood for the first time. For this reason support-group facilitators need to teach and model good boundaries in relationships, and groups need to practice good preventative procedures such as not having lingering conversations in the parking lot following meetings.)
- Cheryl also saw my behavior changing, including seeing me do things like stand up to authority figures for the first time. These things could have resulted in my being out of a job and us being out on the street.

All of these changes concerned her. In her own words, "For a long time I thought recovery might be making things worse."

If a *Family and Friends* group had been available, Cheryl might have been better able to deal with these fears. She could have experienced her own group sharing and the intimacy that goes along with group involvement. She could have processed her fears and feelings in a supportive environment with others who were experiencing the same concerns. Possibly we would have been able to communicate better.

Goals for *Family and Friends*

The following might be called "Goals for *Family and Friends*," or you may see them as the ways to use this material. This set of goals points to some ways such a group can operate.

1. To assist family members and friends to relate better to the person who is working through personal recovery issues.
2. To introduce church members who do not have a recovery background to some of the principles, processes, and language of recovery.
3. To help individuals who are in denial about their own recovery issues to identify and become willing to address those issues.
4. To prevent some divorces or other broken relationships due to the changes brought about by recovery.
5. To assist every person to become willing to practice self-examination and to take responsibility for his or her own actions.

Your Goals for Your *Family and Friends* Group

As you prepare to lead/facilitate a *Family and Friends* group, take time to write below your own goals for yourself and for your group.

Goals for my personal growth:

_____

_____

_____

_____

_____

_____

_____

Goals for my group:

_____

_____

_____

_____

_____

_____

_____

_____

Share your personal and group goals with your co-facilitator. Encourage your co-facilitator also to set goals. Make a note to review these goals after Group Sessions 3, 6, and 9.

Facilitator Qualifications

Family and Friends is a unique type of support group. For some support groups, a highly trained and skilled facilitator is essential. *Shelter from the Storm,* a group dealing with sexual abuse, is an example of this type of support group. Because the issues dealt with in a sexual-abuse recovery group are so personal and painful, the safety of the group members absolutely requires a set of specialized skills. In fact, we recommend that a person facilitating a sexual-abuse group be either a licensed counselor or a person with at least two years in recovery from sexual abuse.

Other support groups need a well trained facilitator but do not require nearly the level of training or expertise of a *Shelter from the Storm* group. *A Time for Healing: Coming to Terms with Your Divorce* is an example of this second type of group. Because a divorce-recovery group operates differently, the facilitator needs to be well prepared, but does not require the level of specialized training that a more intensive group requires.

The facilitator for a *Family and Friends* group is extremely important, but, like *A Time for Healing,* this group facilitator does not require intensive and specialized training. If you have been asked to facilitate a *Family and Friends* group, you can do an excellent job if you will follow some simple guidelines. The following paragraphs describe some of the tasks and criteria for selecting support-group facilitators. As you read them, keep in mind that a *Family and Friends* group is designed to be the most introductory type of group. You do not need to fear that this group will involve difficult psychological concepts or frightening methodology.

Who should facilitate a *Family and Friends* Group?

Due to the unique nature of the *Family and Friends* group, people from a variety of life situations could well become effective facilitators. Possibly the most ideal person would be one who had a family member or friend who was in recovery, experienced difficulty relating to the process, and who has worked through the situation and now is in a good relationship to both the person and the recovery process. Someone who has been in recovery for some time could also be an effective facilitator. Or a person who genuinely wants to understand and relate better to a recovering person could become a facilitator.

Previous Experience

The single most important training to be a support-group facilitator is first to be a participant in a support group. Many of the best support-group ministries around the country follow a strict progression. Before individuals can become leaders or facilitators, they must first participate in a group. Then they must serve as a co-facilitator of a group. Only then can they serve as leaders or facilitators. The problem with this ideal is obvious. You have to have support groups before you can have people who are experienced in support groups. In fact, this need is one of the great strengths of a *Family and Friends* group. *Family and Friends* is an excellent introduction to support-group ministry. Therefore, if you have been asked or are considering facilitating a *Family and Friends* group, I would encourage you first to participate in a group. If that is not possible, the Holy Spirit can make you equal to the task if you will prepare well and depend upon Him.

Facilitator—not Teacher

In spite of the encouragement that a variety of people can be effective facilitators, *Family and Friends* is not a Bible study in which the lecture method is appropriate. In fact, some of the best Bible teachers may not be qualified to lead a support group because they may insist on teaching content rather than facilitating group interaction. The support-group facilitator guides the group process, allows group members to share, and assists members to identify and explore their own feelings about the issues that the group considers.

Spiritual Qualifications

Any leader of a Christ-centered support group should have certain spiritual qualifications. A support-group facilitator should—

- be a Christian with a growing personal relationship with Jesus Christ;
- be a person of prayer and daily Bible study;
- be an active member of a local church;
- have a sense of God's call to the ministry of support groups;
- be spiritually gifted for the work;

- have a commitment to confidentiality within the group;
- be willing to give time and energy to help group members;
- have a teachable spirit;
- love the Lord and love people; and
- be sensitive to the daily leadership of the Holy Spirit.

Persons who have led groups through *Experiencing God, Disciple's Prayer Life,* or *MasterLife* have a strong spiritual foundation for leading support groups. We strongly recommend *LIFE Support Leader's Handbook* (item 7268-02) and *WiseCounsel: Skills for Lay Counseling* (item 7259-08) as resources for potential support-group facilitators. These two resources address in detail issues this introduction mentions.

Additionally, the paragraphs which follow discuss important interpersonal qualifications for a support-group facilitator. As you read them, you may feel overwhelmed at the range of skills this book suggests for a support-group facilitator. Let me reassure you that leading a support group is possible for you.

I suspect you are reading this facilitator's guide because you've sensed a calling to meet the deeply felt needs of people. God would not call you to a task without equipping you to live it out. Remember that the apostle Paul's testimony, "My grace is sufficient for you, for my power is made perfect in weakness" (2 Corinthians 12:9, NIV) can be your testimony, too. You may feel less than adequate in some of these interpersonal skills, but if God has led you to join Him in this ministry, He will give you gifts to do the tasks ahead.

- **Be an effective communicator in sending messages.** Communication involves both verbal and nonverbal skills. The set of your mouth, the look in your eyes, and the tone of your voice all communicate to group members the message you are sending.

Communication specialists tell us—
- only 7 percent of any message is contained in the words the person speaks;
- 38 percent of any message is contained in the tone of voice the person uses; and
- 55 percent of any message is contained in the nonverbal cues surrounding the words a person speaks.

These specialists further tell us that when the verbal message and the nonverbal message clash, the nonverbal message is the one people believe! Intuitively, you know this is true. Ever asked a jaw-clenched, arms-crossed, red-in-the-face person, "Anything wrong?" and heard in reply, "Nothing; I'm fine. Why do you ask?" Moments like these are almost comical. Whether or not your discussion continued, you knew this person and that moment in his life was anything but fine.

Sometimes your role as effective message-sender involves repeating what you hear group members say. Comments like: "What I hear you saying is..." or "Help me understand what you're telling us; are you saying...?" allows you and that group member to communicate accurately during group sessions.

- **Be an effective listener who knows how to hear meanings, not just words.** Your group members will be dealing with critical life issues; they frequently feel a desperate need for someone to hear their story and to understand their pain. Listening is a skill everyone can practice and develop.

Give group members undivided attention when they speak. Keep your eyes focused on the individual speaking. Prevent interruptions. Your chief task as a facilitator may be to help other group members respect the person speaking. Resist the urge to plan your next words while someone speaks.

Occasionally a good listener gives nonverbal feedback—raised eyebrows, nod of the head, a smile, or a sympathetic groan. He may lean forward in a chair, with his arms and hands relaxed and uncrossed—and give verbal feedback—"I understand," "Please continue," or "I know that feeling well."

You may be shocked occasionally by information some group members disclose. Your role is not to communicate judgment or censure or to reinterpret their experiences. Be careful; your nonverbal cues often communicate these attitudes, even if your words do not. Your role is to create a safe place for disclosure and to create a confidential setting in which honesty is the first step toward recovery and healing.

- **Be a servant leader in the group.** A support-group facilitator must be a companion-traveler with group members traveling the road of recovery and spiritual growth. However, the group facilitator also is a traveler who has been on the road longer and who can help interpret the road's markers. Group members need to know that their facilitator empathetically identifies with their struggles to change and still is in the process of change, too.

Most importantly, offer your history and your hope as Jesus did. Jesus was a servant leader who the Scriptures tell us was willing to wash the dirt of recovery's road off the feet of its travelers. You will sometimes fill this function for your group members.

- **Be an encourager to each group member.** Encouragement is essential to the support-group process. During group sessions provide continual encouragement to individual members and to the group itself.

Without encouragement your support-group session will be no more than a simple processing of information from each week's study. Encouragement determines whether group members have the courage to apply that information personally and whether they'll persist when they feel discouraged or overwhelmed by the information they've processed.

No matter what happens during the group's time together, find a way to affirm or encourage its members. For weeks some members may give the group only their presence; affirm their courage to keep coming and keep studying. Some members will be able to tell their stories only with tears; affirm their courage to be honest in the presence of other people.

- **Be skilled in preventing one person from dominating the group.** As you prevent a person from dominating the group, understand why he is doing so. More than likely, he's never felt a safe place or an appropriate time to admit to his wounds or describe his pain. The support group provides these key elements to healing. Some people will rush toward this experience like a dammed-up river finally released rushes toward the river's banks and mouth. When a group member finally tells something he's never told, let the story flow until the powerful rushing of words begins to calm and slow.

When group members engage in lively discussion, however, one person's dominating can damage the group's commitment to accomplishing its work together. Sometimes a gentle interruption which summarizes what the monopolizer has said brings the monologue to a halt. Occasionally you'll need to restate the question or the discussion task; this reinvites the rest of the group to respond. Sometimes, with gentle humor, you'll say: "Jim, you've convinced us how strongly you feel about this! Let's see if another member has strong convictions he or she would like to explain."

- **Know how to be involved personally without relinquishing leadership.** From the first meeting never forget the importance of the group members' seeing you as a fellow struggler. Without dominating, allow the group to know you as one who has faults, failures, and fears just as the other members of the group.

At the same time be attentive to the group's life and process so that each week's work is done. Your primary responsibility is to provide the time and place where group members can share their feelings and where they can develop the skills to communicate with and support one another.

- **Know how to keep all group members involved in the group's life and process.** Remember, you've already noted that lecture is inappropriate for support groups. If you are only comfortable using the lecture method, do not attempt to lead a support group. This group employs a process of sharing information and sharing feelings about that information. It needs the involvement of every group member.

Let group sessions build on the significant work group members do between sessions in their *Family and Friends* members' books. Use teaching suggestions that employ responses from their weekly work. This gives group members words to say which they've already thought through and helps prevent them from being embarrassed by feeling they must answer sensitive questions on the spot.

Study carefully the procedures this book gives for each session. We include these procedures to provide group members with involvement, application, and opportunity to encourage each other. The teaching suggestions will help you with this skill more than anything else.

However, allowing members to share freely is far more important than is sticking legalistically to a plan you develop before the session begins. Group members sometimes come to the session absolutely bursting at the seams to share something that happened in their lives during the past week that relates to the week's content. Be sensitive to this tendency, and be flexible.

Do not criticize group members for the feelings and insights they share, especially when you find yourself disagreeing with them. Use encouragement to correct faulty perceptions group members share. In the same way do not allow other group members to criticize each other. If they do, trust in the group and concern for its members will never develop.

- **Know how and when to refer group members for professional help.** Be sure your referral strategy is in place before you conduct the first group session. With your pastor or another staff member's help, identify appropriate referral persons and agencies in your vicinity. If possible, talk ahead of time to your referral sources about the specific type of services they offer and about such matters as costs, availability, and emergency service.

As the group progresses, certain members may need professional Christian counseling. Some group members may begin the group thinking that only their friend has problems that require recovery. But group members may discover that they have issues with which to deal also. Some group members may begin to recognize serious problems in their own pasts. Be sensitive to your group members' needs to talk with someone about sensitive issues in their lives.

If a situation should arise in which you believe you should make a referral to a counselor, do not suggest during the session that the person should seek counseling. Speak individually and privately with the group member who you believe falls into this category. Share with the group member your impressions about his need for more than the group is able to offer him, and help him make referral choices. Again, the *LIFE Support Leader's Handbook* and the LIFE course *WiseCounsel: Skills for Lay Counseling* contain units dealing with how to refer persons.

- **Help group members understand psychological expressions of biblical truth.** *Family and Friends* places emphasis on helping people experience emotional maturity as they grow spiritually. As a facilitator, you will help group members arrive at a psychological understanding of themselves within the context of biblical truth.

Our emotional health affects our spiritual health. Our spiritual maturity is not complete without emotional maturity. Beware of people who appear spiritually "mature" but who are emotionally ill. Emotional maturity is empty without spiritual maturity. Beware of a person who professes emotional maturity but who lives within a spiritual vacuum.

Sometimes people use religious "talk" to avoid facing emotional problems. Sometimes people do not meet their spiritual needs while they carefully address emotional issues.

As a facilitator, be very careful about using spiritual statements to manipulate group members. An example would be prefacing a statement with "God is telling me to tell you...." Assume that if God is leading you in what you are saying, the people who receive your message will sense God's presence in what you say.

- **Expect the unexpected!** You'll never be able to control every eventuality in planning for group sessions. You won't have that kind of prophetic insight! Expecting the unexpected is your way to commit yourself to the leading of the Holy Spirit.

Plan well each week, but do not adhere to your plans so rigidly that you cannot recognize what God is doing in the group. Moment by moment you must "lean not on your own understanding" (Proverbs 3:5, NIV) so that you can trust the leadership of the Holy Spirit.

Steps for Starting a Group

This section provides guidance for the small-group coordinator, minister of education, or other leader who is organizing a group. If you have been selected to lead a group and this work already has been done, read only steps 1, 3, 4, 9, 10, and 11.

The following steps can help you prepare to minister effectively through this support group.

✎ **Check each of the following steps as you implement them.**

- ❏ Pray
- ❏ Enlist the group's facilitator
- ❏ Enlist a co-facilitator
- ❏ Understand foundational concepts of support groups
- ❏ Determine the logistics
- ❏ Order materials
- ❏ Set fees
- ❏ Determine child-care arrangements
- ❏ Initiate promotional efforts
- ❏ Get started
- ❏ Request Church Study Course credit

Step 1: Pray

Prayer is the essential ingredient for any ministry. God has a vital interest in persons who seek after Him. He already has begun to use LIFE® Support Group Series ministries through the care of local churches to work in the lives of hurting people. Once your church arrives at a sense of calling and a time of decision about providing support-group ministries, your church undoubtedly will be accepting God's invitation to join Him in a work He already is doing.

Support-group facilitators likely will feel the need to pray each week for their group members and for their specific needs. Begin your personal study time and your preparation time for the group sessions with prayer.

Step 2: Enlist the group's facilitator

Study carefully the section on pages 10-13 of this guide on leading a *Family and Friends* group. Consider the spiritual and interpersonal skills discussed in that section.

Suggest that those persons in your church who select group facilitators use this information while they make these decisions. The skills for being a group facilitator are different from the skills for some types of teaching.

This same information would be useful to place in the hands of prospective group facilitators. Encourage them to study it prayerfully as they seek an answer to the invitation to lead.

Step 3: Enlist a co-facilitator

Begin now to pray for one person in each group who will experience the group as a participant but who also could lead a future group. You may want to choose this person from among those who register for the group, or choose someone who appears to have the necessary skills, qualifications, and life experiences to lead a group.

Provide your co-facilitator with a copy of *Family and Friends Facilitator's Guide* (item 7200-24).

Step 4: Understand foundational concepts of support groups

Study carefully the foundational concepts of support groups explained below and through FG page 17. These guiding principles will undergird your work with your group.

- **Members will be asked to make attendance at group sessions a schedule priority.**

The work of the group together and the dynamics which develop between group members are essential parts of the support-group process. These are jeopardized if group members do not consistently attend group sessions.

This group experience may represent the first time in some group members' lives in which they feel secure enough to trust other people and honestly to identify in others' presence their hurts. Inconsistent attendance by group members will only hamper these important benefits to recovery.

- **Members will be asked to sign the covenant.**

During the introductory session, the group facilitator will distribute copies of the *Family and Friends* group covenant found on page 5 of this facilitator's guide. Members will have time to read it and ask any clarifying questions. Indeed, the group members may negotiate together to add an additional statement or make some minor adjustment in the statements given. Full agreement on the covenant is essential.

The covenant establishes boundaries and requirements for the nine-week support group. Once group members agree on its specific details, each member will sign his or her own covenant and the covenants of every group member. By signing the covenants in each other's presence, everyone commits to support the group and to follow the covenant guidelines. These covenants are for members to keep throughout the support group.

- **Members will be asked to participate in the group process.**

A support group is not just a study group focused on information. A support-group experience invites group members to share feelings, emotions, and perceptions about certain concepts and ideas.

Without all group members involved, an empathetic attachment between group members will not develop. As individuals hear other group members contributing to the process of each session, they realize they are not alone in their needs for support and encouragement. Dispelling a sense of loneliness may be the most important accomplishment of any support group.

Fellowship, understanding, commonality, growth—these all are potential benefits of a lively group process. Someone who never has participated in a good small-group experience may have a difficult time comprehending that these benefits will occur.

As group facilitator you cannot promise these benefits because you do not know how the group will develop. You can make a commitment to lead the group in the best way possible and can ask group members to contribute their insights, experiences, questions, and stories to meet their own needs and to build a strong, healthy group.

- **Members will be asked to deal with personal issues as they arise in the group setting.**

A support group will bring focus and attention to certain difficult or dysfunctional relationships that group members face each day. The support group is intended to help members deal from a biblical perspective with these relationships.

Group members cannot meet these goals if they refuse to face personal issues during the group sessions. You may find that group members avoid these personal issues by using a number of defense mechanisms.

Sometimes members refuse to work on issues by "staying in their heads." They deal with the situation intellectually as if they were completing a brain-teaser puzzle. They simply refuse to feel.

At other times group members will become fearful when they get too close to the edge of their feelings. When they begin to feel painful feelings, they may swallow the emotion. Again, they manage to turn off the feelings rather than experience them.

Members sometimes will substitute an acceptable emotion for the emotion they are really feeling. If anger is permitted for them but sadness is not, they will begin to feel grief and then they may transform those feelings of sadness into expressions of anger. The combinations of substitute emotions are limited only by the creativity of group members. Some will substitute concern for someone else for feeling their own emotions. Some will substitute hurt for anger.

You can help members to identify their emotions during such times. Ask the member to identify what he or she is feeling. Sometimes you may need to press the member gently to identify the feelings rather than describing them. You may make an enlarged copy of the feelings poster from FG page 61. At any time in the group sessions you may refer to the feelings poster and ask members to identify what they are feeling.

Although it seems to be a paradox, individuals are less likely to accept the truth, implications, and emotions in personal issues on their own rather than if they do so surrounded by other supportive people who understand such dysfunctional issues and who hear them and help them. Group members lovingly can confront rationalizations and blocked emotions. They lovingly can confront each other when they tend to hide from reality.

Perhaps most importantly, individual members are more likely to hear and apply biblical truth in a group setting than they are during their study time between sessions.

- **Members will be asked to seek professional Christian counseling if the need for this becomes evident.**

Read again the interpersonal qualification concerning referrals listed in the "Facilitator Qualifications," FG pages 10-13. Referral skills are essential because a needy person may have an emotional problem that requires more help than the group can give.

Make the fact clear from the outset that the facilitator's suggestion about professional counseling never is a sign of rejection but a sign of deep care and concern. Help group members to know that if a group member is dealing with emotional problems in the group session, this can dominate the group and can drain the emotional life and strength from the group.

Keep in mind the possibility that a group member with an emotional problem may be in denial about the problem or is oblivious to its danger. Convey to such a person hope, concern, and your continued acceptance; however, firmly describe the need you sense for this person to see a professional Christian counselor. This person may or may not follow your recommendation. At the time of such a conversation, be prepared to give names and phone numbers of competent professionals you found in your referral search before the course began.

As the support-group facilitator, you can kindly ask the individual in need not to return to the support group if you believe his continual participation would be detrimental to the group process. When referring an individual for counseling or talking with an individual about leaving the group, always do so confidentially.

Remember that one of the purposes of a *Family and Friends* group is to help members identify issues with which they need to deal. Therefore other Christ-centered support groups are a primary referral source for *Family and Friends* groups.

For example some members may recognize for the first time that a behavior in their lives actually is an addiction. You may then refer them to a support group dealing with their particular addiction. Such addiction-related groups include the Christ-centered 12-Step groups for eating disorders (an unhealthy, addictive relationship to food), chemical dependency (alcohol or other drugs), or codependency (an unhealthy, addictive relationship to controlling, rescuing, and fixing other people). Other addiction-related groups include nicotine dependency and sexual addiction.

Some *Family and Friends* members will identify the need to deal with unresolved grief over losses in their lives, or to deal with unresolved childhood issues, or to process the results of sexual abuse. In each of these cases your church or another church in your area may offer Christ-centered support groups to assist individuals with recovery.

You may need to assist members to prioritize their recovery needs. A person cannot and should not deal with several issues at once. For example a woman who is dangerously underweight due to anorexia may also have an addiction to medications, a serious problem with shame, an addiction to nicotine, and be a survivor of sexual abuse. In such cases the person needs to determine which issue is most immediate. In this example the anorexia may be the most life threatening. This woman needs to get immediate professional care. After she has become stabilized in her eating disorder she can then begin to deal with the less life-threatening issues.

Since thinking in the extremes—sometimes called black-and-white thinking—is a characteristic many people struggle with, individuals with multiple recovery issues often think they must solve every problem at once. Do not attempt to counsel people beyond your abilities, but by helping them to see that they can break their issues down into manageable bites, you can assist them to find help. You can assist them to determine which issues to tackle first.

- **Members will maintain confidentiality.**

Trust among group members is an essential element of the support-group process. During the first weeks of your group's discussions, stress confidentiality. Highlight the place of confidentiality in the covenant as an indication of its importance, and insist that a violation of confidentiality is sufficient reason to ask a group member to leave the group permanently.

Sometimes group members break confidentiality without realizing they are doing so. Sharing matters from the group, even as a prayer request, violates the group's confidentiality. Only legal issues such as threats of harm or suicide are adequate reason to break confidentiality.

- **Members will be open to a Christ-centered approach to support in a small-group setting.**

Unchurched individuals and/or non-Christians may well be attracted to your church's ministry through support groups. It is only fair to make clear to such people the focus of your support group.

Encourage these individuals to be open to a Christ-centered approach which keeps Christ at the center of all that the group does or says. A Christ-centered approach to discovering the truth about self, others, and the relationships between them is the way to deal with difficult life issues.

Finally, pray about the possibility that one or more group members may become Christians as they participate in a *Family and Friends* group. Pray that the witness of Scripture and the witness of your life and testimony will speak to those who do not know Christ.

Day 5 in unit 5 of the member's book explains how to become a Christian. This unit presents the gospel in the context of understanding guilt and shame. The explanation of salvation occurs partway through the material for an important reason. By this time in the group's life, as group facilitator, you will be aware of group members who are not Christians. Be especially in prayer for these members as they study unit 5; consider contacting them during that week to invite them to meet your Savior and accept Him as their Lord.

- **Members will abide by the boundaries and guidelines set by the group.**

Each support group sets its own boundaries and guidelines for dealing with such issues as: type of language allowed; absenteeism; refreshments; smoking; member participation; course credit; or length of group sessions.

Before any group begins, plan to consult about such issues with your pastor, church staff members, coordinator of support-group ministries, or any other person, group, or council overseeing your church's support groups. The church may establish guidelines that deal with these matters. Church leaders likely will want you to share these guidelines with your support group as the group is negotiating boundaries and guidelines.

Step 5: Determine the logistics

A facilitator may schedule support groups to meet at any time. If anonymity needs are high, consider scheduling your group's sessions during a time the church is free of all other activities.

Arrange for the group to meet in the same place each week and in a location away from the normal flow of other church activity. Select a distraction-free setting which will not hinder sharing among group members. Look for comfortable, movable furniture, and check on adequate lighting, heating, and cooling of the room.

Establish a clearly understood starting time. As a group, plan to decide on the length of each session. The minimum amount of time is one hour to one and a half hours; a two-hour session will eliminate the feeling of hurry and will allow more in-depth exploration of each unit's content.

Step 6: Order materials

Order sufficient copies of the following materials well in advance of your first meeting.

- *Family and Friends: Helping the Person You Care About in Recovery* (item 7200-26; ISBN 0-8054-9872-9), one for each group member, facilitator, and co-facilitator.

- *Family and Friends: Helping the Person You Care About in Recovery Facilitator's Guide* (item 7200-24; ISBN 0-8054-9871-0), one guide for each facilitator and co-facilitator. You can buy these at local Baptist Book Stores or Lifeway Christian Stores, or you can order these from the Customer Service Center; 127 Ninth Avenue, North; Nashville, TN 37234; 1-800-458-2772.

Step 7: Set fees

Typically, the fee for a support group covers the cost of the member's book. You may want to charge more than that amount for such costs as providing scholarships for those who cannot afford a book, buying the leadership materials, buying refreshments, or providing child care.

Your church may subsidize a portion of the cost of the books, and the fee for the group becomes less than the book costs. The fee still is important because—
- it immediately establishes a level of commitment of time and resources to join the group; and
- it allows group members to feel they are contributing something to the support-group ministry.

However, do not use fees to pay the group's facilitator. Support groups are lay-led, not professionally-led groups. This important detail will help protect your church from legal liability.

Step 8: Determine child-care arrangements

Decide before promotion begins whether your church will offer child care for group members' children. Such a service is essential for some people to join your group. Certainly cost of child care is important to consider. Sometimes group sessions do not wrap up at the same time each week. This is difficult for children and child-care providers alike.

Step 9: Initiate promotional efforts

Schedule at least a three-week period for promotion and registration for the support group. Clearly state that the group will be closed. This means that no one is allowed to join after the first session. NOTE: Enroll no more than 8 to 10 members in each support group.

Determine your target audience. The most obvious target group for *Family and Friends* is the spouses or close friends of people who are in your church's support-group ministry. On FG page 58 you will find a sample letter you could send to these individuals advising them of the group. You need, however, to observe confidentiality regarding the people who are involved in groups. You might circulate the sample letter on FG page 58 to the people in your existing support groups, asking them if they have a friend or loved one who they would like to see involved in a *Family and Friends* group. In that way you can both determine those who are prospective members of a *Family and Friends* group and you can obtain permission from their recovering friend. Under no circumstances should you contact the friends of persons who are in support groups without those persons' permission.

In addition to inviting those who have had friends involved in the church's support-group ministry, you likely will want to extend an opportunity for others to be involved. Following the sample letter on FG page 58 are two additional sample letters to be sent to prospective participants. Because the focus of a support group differs from that of a discovery group, you will find a sample letter for both prospective target audiences.

If you plan to target only church members, use the normal channels of promotion in your church, such as the church's newsletter, posters, or bulletin inserts. See FG page 62 for ideas. Your pastor could preach one or several sermons from Luke 4:18-19, which describes Jesus' healing ministry. Chapter 1 of the *LIFE Support Leader's Handbook* provides a sample sermon. If the pastor supports the support-group ministry, this enables many people to bless the ministry even if they never participate in any support group. If the pastor supports a support-group ministry, members of the congregation will see groups as an extension of Jesus' ministry.

If you plan an enlistment campaign outside your church, then promote the group by using free publicity like public-service announcements or notices on your newspaper's religion page. Your church can print posters inexpensively and can ask church members to post these notices in their places of business. See FG page 62 for ideas. A small card or brochure about support groups can be part of your church's visitor's packet or during outreach visits in homes. Many churches have found a support-group ministry to be a tremendous outreach option for their church.

Once groups have begun, word will begin to spread person-to-person about their benefits. Inquiries likely will start. Keep an accurate waiting list of those wanting a place in the next group.

Chapter 3 of the *LIFE Support Leader's Handbook* offers many suggestions for promoting LIFE® Support Group Series courses inside and outside the church. Designate someone in the church office to deal with inquiries about future support groups. Make certain the person designated is knowledgeable about the subject. All publicity, in or outside the church, can list a phone number to call for more information.

Step 10: Get started

Review the nine steps in this overview to ensure you've covered all necessary details. Read through the first three units of the member's book and the facilitator's guide. This will help you become familiar with the material and the basic outline of group sessions.

Schedule a meeting with your co-facilitator to review details. Study together the first unit in the member's book and facilitator's guide, and plan your first group session. Decide whether or not you will use the support-group approach or the discovery-group approach. Plan accordingly if you intend to offer the optional introductory session.

When planning weekly group sessions, you'll find more suggestions for discussion than your group members can complete during a session. Select the activities you believe are most relevant to your group's needs.

The introductory meeting for your support group is the time to distribute member's books, discuss the group covenant, and introduce participants to the LIFE® Support Group Series course format. You also may choose to provide a brief course overview as participants acquaint themselves with their members' books and as you lead members through an overview of the course map on the inside back cover of their books. Highlighting with the group members the unit page for each unit provides a good summary of each unit's content.

Step 11: Request Church Study Course credit

Group members who complete the course of study for *Family and Friends: Helping the Person You Care About in Recovery* are eligible for study course credit from the Baptist Sunday School Board. During the last session, members need to fill out the Church Study Course form on FG page 64. Copy one for each member. Be sure to sign your name where appropriate.

After the forms are completed, mail them to Church Study Course Awards Office; Baptist Sunday School Board; 127 Ninth Avenue, North; Nashville, TN 37234. Read the information on FG page 63, become familiar with the Church Study Course system, and learn more about how to request study course credit for *Family and Friends*.

How to Succeed as a Leader

Please read the following material carefully. It will help to assure your success as a facilitator for a Family and Friends group.

Imagine yourself going into a baseball game with the advance knowledge that no matter how many runs the other team scored, your team soon would score one more. As you begin to lead the *Family and Friends* group, you can have the same kind of certainty of success.

The LIFE learning system is just that—a learning system. It is not a teaching system. We base the LIFE learning system on a process we call "writing for life change." If the group members read the material and complete the written learning activities, they will learn more than a teacher ever will be able to hammer into their heads.

You cannot *teach* this material. No matter how much you want to do so, you cannot change the lives of your group members. You probably will begin to see areas of your group members' lives that you would like to change, but you cannot do so. As a facilitator you cannot take the place of the Holy Spirit in group members' lives.

"Guaranteed" Success

How can you succeed as a group facilitator? View yourself as an encourager. Your purpose is to help the group members to grow. Place the responsibility for learning and growing where it belongs—on the group members. Develop your own boundaries so that you recognize that the responsibility for change remains with the group member. Seek to avoid placing yourself in the position of feeling responsible for the progress group members do or do not make.

You may sometimes feel like a referee for the group. Group members will not initially understand how to function as a group. They will not understand how to respect each others' boundaries. They may disrespect each other by interrupting, by not listening when another member speaks, or by giving inappropriate advice. Your job will be to train the members in how to function as a group. If a group member tramples the boundaries of another group member in one of the ways mentioned above, tactfully but clearly explain that the group functions like a healthy family. Explain the boundary violation—without shaming the person who committed the offense—then allow the group process to continue.

The One Goal

When I lead a support group, I have a single goal. Whether or not anything else is accomplished, I plan to do this one thing. I will encourage group members toward the goal. To the degree that doing so is possible, I will seek to hold them accountable. I plan group sessions by summarizing the material and asking good discussion questions. Sometimes I have to practice group management skills to keep someone from dominating the group or trampling on the boundaries of other group members, but in everything I strive for the one purpose. That single purpose is to see that the group member completes the written work in the member's book.

Group members do not work the activities simply by reading a book. They need to interact with the member's book. By doing so, they actually will be doing the work of self-discovery and spiritual growth. They will be reflecting on the material and making life-changing decisions. Individual reflection and application are the bases for change.

Then Why Participate in a Group?

If the personal work is so important, then why have a group at all? Several reasons exist for why the group is so important.

You will find that as group members do the activities in the member's book, they will discover concepts and truths that they will need to process with the group members. They will learn the importance of growth in the relational area of their lives. Their work in the member's book will lead them to participation in the group. The group time then becomes alive and interactive.

Many of us also need the group for encouragement. Group meetings provide the incentive to complete the written work. Few people would faithfully complete their work without the accountability and encouragement the group provides.

So when I lead a support group, I have a single goal—to encourage the group members to complete their work in the member's book. I hope to encourage members as they learn, but they do the work of learning. When the group members understand and commit themselves to this concept, the group meetings become times of rich sharing about what God is doing in the members' lives. Individual work accomplishes a great deal during the week. Whatever happens in the group meeting is an extra bonus.

Sometimes you may have a week when nothing goes right. You may feel that everything you did as a facilitator fell flat as a potato chip on the freeway at rush hour. In that moment place the responsibility for growth back where it belongs—with the group members.

A Subtle Danger

Be aware that if we adopt a "teacher" mentality, this actually can become an obstacle to growth. If we concentrate on doing a good job presenting the material, we may excuse the group members from their responsibilities. Unconsciously our goal becomes to impress them. We serve our group members more effectively if we clearly place the responsibility for learning where it belongs—on their shoulders.

Does this mean leadership is easy or unimportant? No, it does not. We can spend the rest of our lives improving our skills as group facilitators. What it does mean is that the Holy Spirit is in charge; I can relax and pay attention to people rather than worrying about content.

I wish you well as you lead your group members through *Family and Friends*. You will succeed according to the Lord's purposes if you pray for your group members, encourage them, and participate actively.

A Word About Methodology

As you use this facilitator's guide you will find that we have divided each unit by days. We intend that this division will help you find the related information and activities in the member's book. The division is for convenience only. It does not mean that you will use only one day per week or that you must follow a particular order. Choose from the suggested discussion starters and activities those that will best help your group members to process the information in the unit. Then use the activities in the way and order that best fits your group.

How to Lead/Facilitate the Group

This facilitator's guide deliberately attempts to avoid telling you specifically how to guide the group. You will get to know the personalities and needs of your group members. You will pray regularly for their needs. The Holy Spirit may lead you to deal differently with the group than what I would suggest.

You will do well if you observe the following guidelines.

1. Complete the unit for yourself. Do the activities as a participant. Groups are not classes. No place exists in groups for a "teacher" who is a detached authority figure. Even if you have experience and knowledge about the topics in the member's book, complete the study for yourself. Groups are uniquely confessional. Confessional means more than confessing our sins. Confessional means we share our own experience. We do not simply share content or ideas. We share ourselves.

2. Out of the unit choose the key concepts or ideas that you believe are most important. Design activities and questions that will lead members to deal with these central themes of the unit. You may use the activities and questions provided in the Group Session materials or you may choose to create your own. Either way, the object needs to be to encourage the members to interact with the concepts and issues in the unit.

3. Always plan more activities or sharing starters than you will need. Then when you begin a session you may do so with confidence. If members do not respond to an issue you may move on to another activity, but note that silence is valuable in a group. Do not feel that you must keep something going every minute. Sometimes you may ask a question or ask people to share on a topic and none of the members may respond. They may be deciding how the issue affects their lives. They may be afraid to speak first. Do not fill the silence with chatter or rush on to the next topic. You can teach the group to permit silence.

4. Expect to have unfinished business. If you feel that you must "complete the lesson," you may miss some of the most important moments of support-group life. Learn to value the group members more highly than the premium you put on covering content. Regarding item 3 above, plan more than you need, and plan to fail to cover all that you prepared.

5. Model the role. You cannot expect group members to have the courage to share the personal aspects of their lives if you do not. *Modeling the role* means sharing something of your own human failures. It means confessing your sins so that those you lead will have the courage to confess their sins. Modeling the role says to members, "We have come to talk honestly about _____ and I will begin by sharing myself honestly."

6. Relax and listen. The greatest gift you can give to those in your group is your attention, not your answers. When others struggle, you may feel compelled to solve their problems. You may feel that others expect you to have the answers to their dilemmas. If you follow those urgings, you will become more interested in the content and in the members' opinions of you than in your group members as individuals. You do not have to provide answers. In fact, most of the time you will do more harm than good by providing answers, even if the answers are good, true, and correct.

When you feel the need to provide an answer, remind yourself how you feel when others give you answers instead of giving you their attention. Remind yourself that whenever you provide answers you are also delivering a powerful put-down. You are saying in effect, "You are not capable of solving your own answers, you need me to provide solutions for you." Then listen. Make providing a safe environment for sharing your first priority in the group.

7. Lead the members to share themselves. Always maintain that goal for yourself—to use activities, to use group management skills, to use good questions, all for the single purpose of getting members to share themselves. Note the difference between members sharing their ideas, knowledge, or thoughts and members sharing *themselves*. The group has been a tremendous success whenever members have talked honestly about their fears, faults, and feelings. When they talk about those issues, they come to understand themselves more clearly and they become able to relate to God and others more effectively.

8. Keep the group Christ-centered rather than religious. In a religious group people are concerned with the correct answers. They want to appear suitably holy. In a Christ-centered meeting, people are honest and real. They do not seek religious clichés. They honestly seek to know Christ more deeply.

Grace and joy to you on the journey.

Support or Discovery Group?

You read about the types of LIFE® Support Group Series groups on FG pages 6-7. Discovery groups are for a general audience. They are for anyone interested in learning about the topic of the group. A *group leader* guides a discovery group. Support groups are for a specialized audience. They are only for persons who identify the issue of the group in their own lives. A group *facilitator* guides a support group.

When we first made plans for *Family and Friends*, the only intention was for a support group. The purpose was limited to helping the spouse, family member, or close friend of the person who was experiencing recovery. The goal was to help that friend relate better to the changes and challenges he or she was experiencing. However, as the manuscript for the member's book came together, another value for *Family and Friends* became apparent. We began to see that this could be an excellent introduction to support-group ministry.

Many Christians have a heart to minister to hurting people, but they have difficulty relating fully to the hurts and distorted perceptions that come from life experiences like alcoholism or abuse. These church members need a chance to study and understand how a support group operates. Because we all have hurts and sins, some of those persons also need a chance to identify the issues in their own lives with which they need to deal.

Family and Friends can provide the basis for such a discovery-group experience. A discipleship leader, pastor, educational director, or small groups coordinator of a church may use *Family and Friends* as an introduction to how support groups work.

Because of the possible dual purpose for this resource, we have provided a two-track approach to leadership. You will see that the group sessions contain goals and introductory information about each session. Then the "During the Session" portion of each unit is presented in three parts.

The first division of "During the Session" is the suggested support-group lesson plan. If you are unsure about how to facilitate the support-group session, you may take the suggested lesson plan and use it. You will see that we have done just what we suggested in the previous paragraphs. We have selected the learning activities and planned for a typical group. Just as suggested, we have planned more than you will probably need. In facilitating a session, we would feel no need to cover all the suggested activities.

The second portion of the "During the Session" is the suggested discovery-group lesson plan. In this session we have suggested how we would approach the session with a typical discovery group.

The third portion of "During the Session" is the suggested leadership helps for the session listed by the days of the unit. As a facilitator, you know your group best. We encourage you to select the sharing activities from this portion and plan the weekly session to fit your group. Prayerfully select more activities than you think you need. As a result you can go into the group session with confidence that you do not have to do all the talking. You can explain an activity and then allow the group to share and discuss the issue. If you have more planned than you need, you do not have to cover all the material. Your goal can be to lead the members to share and process what they have been learning as they did the work during the week.

We hope that the three-part presentation will provide you the maximum flexibility along with specific help on how to facilitate or lead your group.

Opportunities and Challenges

As a facilitator/leader of a *Family and Friends* group you have a unique set of opportunities and challenges which grow out of the distinctive make-up of a *Family and Friends* group. If your support-group members have a family member or friend who is in recovery, a great temptation will exist to spend the group time "taking the other person's inventory." The phrase *taking someone's inventory* refers to the practice of concentrating on the faults and failures of others as a way to avoid dealing with our own deficiencies.

Our sin nature seems particularly drawn to the approach of blaming the other person while avoiding our own faults, sins, weaknesses, and failures. Blaming others is the most frequently used method of avoiding personal responsibility and, therefore, avoiding change. A key part of the leadership task of a *Family and Friends* group leader/facilitator is to help group members avoid "taking someone else's inventory."

If you are leading a discovery group, the temptation will not be as great to blame the other person. In this setting, the temptation may be to intellectualize by talking only about the abstract principles without ever making personal application.

A major portion of your task as facilitator/leader is to encourage group members to apply the material to themselves. You will work to overcome the twin hazards of blaming and gossip on the one hand and intellectual avoidance on the other.

Dr. John Drakeford, counseling professor at Southwestern Baptist Theological Seminary, taught an effective counseling method to deal with the problem of blaming others. He would say: "Now Mr. Jones, how much of this problem is because of your wife's behavior and how much is because of your behavior?" He would then negotiate to arrive at a supposed percentage of blame. "Do you suppose that the problem is 90% your wife's fault? Well, even though the problem is 90% your wife's fault, since she is not here, and you are... Tell me about the 10% that is your responsibility."

As you guide the group, you will need to develop the skill that Dr. Drakeford taught. You can do so with both directness and grace. Explain to the group members that neither the material nor the group is suggesting that anything is "wrong" with them. Explain that this process is not about placing blame on the guilty party but about finding solutions to difficult situations.

Enlist the group members' assistance by stating: "Because of the unique nature of our group, I will need your help. In other types of groups, the members come together because they seek to deal with and overcome a problem in their lives; therefore, they restrict the discussion in the group to each person talking about his or her own issues. We call this using "I" messages rather than "you" messages. In our *Family and Friends* group we come together not primarily because of a problem we recognize in our own lives. We come together to learn how to understand and deal with our friend's recovery. This unique make-up of the group is the reason I need your help. We may be tempted to focus on our friend or family member, but we accomplish little by dissecting the other person and his or her problem. Instead, in this group, we will seek to understand our friends by imitating their recovery process.

In other Christ-centered support groups the individual talks only about himself and his contribution to the issue or problem. We will talk about *ourselves* and *our* contribution to the issue or problem.

In other groups, the person seeks to get in touch with her feelings. We will seek to get in touch with *our* feelings.

In other groups members confess their sins, not the sins of others. In our group we will confess *our* sins, not the sins of others.

In other groups members seek to learn about and practice healthy and Christ-honoring boundaries. We will do the same. Please help me to keep our group on this track."

Not the "No Talk" Rule

That we keep the emphasis on ourselves does not mean that we return to the "no talk" rule of the dysfunctional family. Sometimes we need to talk about the behaviors of other persons, but in a healthy group the emphasis remains on our own thoughts, feelings, and actions.

Explain to your group that this temptation to talk about the other person is self-defeating for the following reasons.

1. To violate the other person's boundaries by simply gossiping about him or her is inappropriate. This principle does not mean that we are following the "no talk" rule. A difference exists between keeping family secrets and gossip. Gossip is talking about another person in an attempt to make myself look or feel better. Sometimes we need to relate what another person said or did, but we need to monitor our own motives carefully. Are we sharing to understand the situation and to take responsibility for our own actions? Or are we telling about another person's irresponsibility to gain sympathy or to avoid dealing with our own behaviors?

2. We need to keep the focus on ourselves during this group because we learn best by doing. We could talk about how other support groups operate, but we will learn far more by actually doing what those groups do.

3. We seek to understand and practice good boundaries. Boundaries are the "invisible fences" God has given us to protect ourselves from abuse by others and to keep us from abusing them. We cannot practice good boundaries by violating the boundaries of others.

A Difficult Issue

The problem of balance between gossip and keeping family secrets is difficult in any group. As facilitator/leader of a *Family and Friends* group, be aware that this will be a problem for the group. Seek to model for the group the principle of individual responsibility. As you gain skills as a facilitator, you will both gain skills in this area and you will make mistakes—that is why recovery is a process.

Preparation for Unit 1

Optional Introductory Session

Session Goals

In this optional introductory session group members will—
- begin to form a group relationship as they share basic information about themselves;
- make any necessary adjustments to the group covenant and together commit themselves to the group by signing the covenant;
- obtain their copies of the *Family and Friends* member's book if they do not already have one.

What to Expect

Depending on the make-up of the group, you may have individuals who have no idea what a support group is, people who have strange concepts of a support group, those who feel considerable fear and tension about being present, and/or people who look forward to the group with great anticipation. This first group session will be very important as members begin to build relationships of trust.

Before the Session

- ❑ If you are providing child care, confirm arrangements. Because the first session may run a little longer than other sessions, make sure that workers are prepared to stay as late as necessary.
- ❑ Check the church calendar to make sure that you have the room requested and for the length of time needed. You do not want people arriving for another meeting as you are completing your group time.
- ❑ Contact group members to make sure they know when and where you are meeting. This will also give you an opportunity to respond to last-minute questions and anxious reservations.
- ❑ Make sure the room is clean and chairs are arranged in a circle with just enough to accommodate your group. Remember to leave a gap in the circle of chairs and do not place a chair in front of the door. Avoid creating a feeling of being trapped.
- ❑ Provide several boxes of tissues.
- ❑ Have tear sheets and markers available for use during the session.
- ❑ Prepare two copies of the group covenant for each member of the group.
- ❑ If you are using a support-group approach, prepare one copy of Handout 1, "My Identity," for each member of the group.
- ❑ If you are using a discovery-group approach, prepare one copy of Handout 2, "Our Relationship-Recovery Story," for each member of the group.
- ❑ Prepare your relationship-recovery story if you have one. If you cannot share your own recovery testimony for whatever reason, tell Dale and Cheryl's story from FG page 8. Make your testimony a maximum of five minutes in length. Seek to include these elements:
  - how I or my friend began recovery;
  - how I or my friend felt (fearful, abandoned, left-out); and
  - the fact that we have and are working through the issues (that hope exists).

  Do not attempt to explain how you and your friend have worked out the difficulties—that is the purpose of the entire course—but do give encouragement that relationships can survive and grow through the support-group experience.
- ❑ As you plan and lead the group session, be careful to reserve 10-15 minutes at the end of the time to review and sign the group covenant.

During the Session

Arrival—Greet the group members as they arrive for the session. Invite them to sit in the circle.

Start—Set an example by beginning on time.
- Ask: "What do you hope to receive from this group?" Ask someone to record one- or two-word summaries of the responses on the flip chart. Remove this sheet and place it on the wall with masking tape.
- Ask: "What do you hope to accomplish in this group?" Record these responses on another flip chart sheet. Remove this sheet and place it on the wall with masking tape.

Take only a few minutes for these two preliminary questions. This will allow opportunity for group members to begin to feel comfortable in the group before moving to the next segment of the group time—sharing personal history.

Sharing for Support Group

If you are using *Family and Friends* to introduce the members to the support-group process, explain that sharing our personal history is a building block of any support group. State that you will take a portion of this meeting to get to know each member. Begin by briefly sharing your personal history, dreams, and emotions and then allow an opportunity for each member to share. State: "By sharing about ourselves we will begin not only to become a group but individually to gain intimacy skills."

Distribute Handout 1, "My Identity" to group members. Share your own responses. Lead the group members to share the issues regarding their various identities. Stress that each person should share only that level of intimacy with which they feel safe.

Sharing for Discovery Group

As the primary sharing portion of the meeting, explain that you will each share your recovery-relationship story. Distribute copies of Handout 2, "Our Relationship-Recovery Story." Model the process by sharing the testimony you prepared before the group meeting—either Dale and Cheryl's story or your own. Lead the members to share their stories.

Group Covenant

Distribute copies of the group covenant; two per member. Lead the group members in a brief discussion of the covenant. Explain that for the group to function we must each make a serious commitment to the group process. Lead the group members to sign both copies of the group covenant. They will each retain one copy of the covenant and turn in one copy to the facilitator. If necessary, and with group consensus, make any additions or changes to the covenant.

While enforcement of the covenant should always be a matter of grace, I would strongly urge you not to minimize the importance of the group covenant. Those groups that choose to disregard the covenant almost inevitably suffer for it.

Closing and Prayer

Use the signing of the group covenant as a time of commitment together to the group process. State that in the coming weeks your group will be learning important information but also will be developing valuable relationships. Lead the group in prayer. You may choose to end by reciting the "Serenity Prayer."

*God, grant me the serenity to accept the things
I cannot change, courage to change the things I can,
and the wisdom to know the difference.*[1]

After the Session

❑ Write down each group member's name and phone number. Before the next group session, pray for each member specifically. Pray for members with special needs.
❑ Call each group member. Encourage him or her in the preparation for the next session.
❑ Read "Before the Session" for Group Session 1, and carefully complete all the activities in unit 1 of the member's book.
❑ Meet with your co-facilitator.
Establish a regular meeting time with him or her for the following three purposes. Meet together to—
  1. debrief from the previous session. Discuss the group dynamics and any special needs of group members.
  2. plan for the next session.
  3. pray for group members and for yourselves as you lead.
Be sensitive in sharing if your co-facilitator is a group member. This is not a gripe session between the two of you but is an opportunity for encouragement and support.
Be sure your co-facilitator has a copy of the Facilitator's Guide (item 7200-24).

---

[1]Reinhold Neibuhr, "The Serenity Prayer," (St. Meinrad, IN: Abbey Press).

Group Session 1: Support Group Life

> **Session Goals**
>
> Group members will—
> - gain an understanding of what takes place in a support group;
> - discover why a support group is so vital and valuable for the recovery process;
> - learn how to cooperate instead of compete with the support-group process.

What to Expect

Depending on the make-up of the group, you may have individuals who have no idea what a support group is, people who have strange concepts of a support group, those who feel considerable fear and tension about being present, and/or people who look forward to the group with great anticipation.

If you conducted an introductory session, the members have begun to bond as a group by sharing portions of their histories or identities with one another. If this is your first group session, give attention to basic group building. Look over the suggested sharing from the optional introductory session. You may want to use some of those activities in this session.

Beware of a special problem in a *Family and Friends* group. Since the person in the group is present because of a relationship with another person, gossip is an ever-present danger. From the very beginning, you will need to help members identify the difficult line between studying and sharing about a relationship in order to understand and solve problems on the one hand and violating the other person's boundaries, breaking confidences, and blaming on the other.

Before the Session

❑ Read and complete the learning activities for unit 1 in *Family and Friends* member's book.
❑ Confirm child-care provisions for the group if the church is providing child care.
❑ Check the church calendar to make sure that you have the room requested and for the length of time requested. You do not want people arriving for another meeting as you are completing your group time.
❑ Contact group members to make sure they know when and where you are meeting. This will also give you an opportunity to respond to last-minute questions and anxious reservations.
❑ Make sure the room is clean and chairs are arranged in a circle with just enough to accommodate your group. Remember to leave a gap in the circle of chairs and do not place a chair in front of the door. Avoid creating a feeling of being trapped.
❑ Provide several boxes of tissues.
❑ Have tear sheets and markers available for use during the session.
❑ If you did not conduct an introductory session, prepare two copies of the group covenant for each member of the group. Refer to FG page 27 for help in leading members to sign the covenant.
❑ Make necessary posters and copies of Handout 3, "Levels of Sharing."

During the Session

Arrival—Greet the group members as they arrive for the session.

Start—Set an example by beginning on time.
- Introduce yourself. Tell the group how you became the facilitator of this group. If you did not share your recovery-relationship story last week you may do so at this time.
- Ask the group members to introduce themselves.

The following activities and discussion suggestions are organized by the lessons in the unit to help you better find the material in the member's book. However, in preparing and facilitating the group session, disregard the lesson divisions. Simply select the activities and discussion topics you need to guide the group as they process the week's material. Remember that I have provided far more material than you can possibly cover in a single session. Select the suggestions that will work for you and for your group.

Suggested Support-Group Lesson Plan

For a support-group type of session, use the suggestions under day 1 in which the facilitator reviews the four sharing styles in families and the group members identify and share the style of their friend's family and their own family of origin. Use the follow-up questions to deepen the sharing as time will allow.

Suggested Discovery-Group Lesson Plan

If you are leading a group of individuals who want to learn about the support-group process, explain that unit 1 is extremely important to understanding support groups. Explain that groups provide people—often for the first time in their lives—with the opportunity to experience genuine, healthy intimacy.

Display a poster or tear sheet of the four levels of sharing (p. 12). Explain that God's plan was that we have emotionally healthy families in which we would learn to share appropriately at each of the four levels. State that since many people have not had adequate opportunity to develop those skills, a support group can provide that opportunity. Ask members to describe if they often long for but also fear sharing at the deepest level. Ask: "Why do we have such difficulty with intimate sharing?"

Explain that a support group helps members to reach the level of intimate sharing by progressing through the four-part process described in day five: *sharing, affirmation, goal setting,* and *genuine community* (pp. 20-22). Display a poster or tear sheet with the four steps. Lead the group to discuss how each of these steps occur in the group. Ask members to share how they have or have not experienced the four steps in their own lives.

Suggested Leadership Helps

Day 1: Why Friends Don't Share, Part 1
Relate Larry Pillow's story from page 9 or share your own similar story. Ask members to think about what reasons or influences cause them to have difficulty sharing how they feel (learning activity on p. 9). Tell why you find sharing emotions difficult. Allow group members to share their responses.

Explain that different patterns for sharing emotions exist in different families (pp. 10-11). Lead the group to brainstorm different styles of dealing with emotions. Stress that you are not seeking the correct answer but simply are seeking to list as many models of sharing as possible. On a chalkboard or tear sheet list the responses. Seek to lead the group to list and describe at least the following possible styles or models.
1. The closed family. Certain or all emotions are discouraged or forbidden.
2. The family where emotions are shown through actions rather than expressed verbally (i.e. Dad would buy me something to say "I'm sorry.").
3. Compulsive. Members deal with emotions by acting out a compulsive behavior.
4. Verbal. The family talks about what they were or are feeling.

After the group has identified as many styles of dealing with emotions as possible, ask members to describe the way feelings were shared in their families of origin and in the family of origin of their friend.

Next ask the members to describe how it would feel to live in a family with a different style of sharing emotions. Caution members that this is not a time to blame. Encourage them that this is a preliminary type of goal-setting exercise. If they choose a different style of sharing, they can begin to work toward developing the skills to make positive change.

Ask the question from page 10, "What feelings do you have difficulty sharing today?" Allow time for responses.

Relate the material on the pain of past failures from pages 10-11. Share how past pain has shaped your ability to trust and to share. Invite members to share.

Day 2: Why Friends Don't Share, Part 2
Lead a discussion of the four levels of sharing. Remind the group that they answered the questions on pages 12-13 about the level of communication they most often experience with their friend. Lead the group to brainstorm ways that they can make it safer for their friends to share with them (p. 13). Record the responses on the chalkboard or tear sheet.

Day 3: Motivating Factors for Sharing
Explain that the inner pain of loneliness motivates us to share our inner selves with someone. One major benefit of a support group is that it gives us a safe place to learn to share ourselves with others. Share how your friend has changed since becoming part of a support group (p. 16). Share also changes you anticipate happening or need to make as a result of participating in a support group. Lead the group to list the changes—both good and bad—they have seen in themselves or in friends. Then discuss and list positive ways to deal with these changes (p. 16).

Day 4: How Support Groups Help
Ask: "Have you ever felt angry, hurt, or left out because your friends have shared with their support group things that they have not shared with you?" Suggest that many friends or spouses of recovering people sometimes feel these emotions. They also sometimes "mind-read" and ascribe all manner of motives to explain why the friend shares more with the group than with them. Relate Helen's story from page 17. Explain that the desire to help others is a motivation to share. Invite members to share their response to the learning activity on page 18 describing how they feel about the friend being "able to share something with a support group that he or she has never been able to share with you."

Day 5: The Support-Group Process
Display a poster or tear sheet with the four parts of the support-group process: *sharing, affirmation, goal setting,* and *genuine community*. Share something of your journey with the process. For example, you might share how you first experienced each of the stages of the process.

After the Session

❏ If you did not have an introductory session, write down each group member's name and phone number.
❏ Pray for each member of the group. Pray for members with special needs.
❏ During the next week, call each group member. Encourage him or her in the preparation for the next session.
❏ Read "Before the Session" for Group Session 2, and carefully complete all the activities in unit 2 of the member's book.
❏ If you choose to use the method described under discovery-group lesson plan on page 31 for the next session, invite the guest couple in advance and explain the process to them.
❏ If you did not have an introductory session, meet for the first time with your co-facilitator.
Establish a regular meeting time with him or her for the following three purposes. Meet together to—
  1. debrief from the previous session. Discuss the group dynamics and any special needs of group members.
  2. plan for the next session.
  3. pray for group members and for yourselves as you lead.
Be sensitive in sharing if your co-facilitator is a group member. This is not a gripe session between the two of you but is an opportunity for encouragement and support.

Be sure your co-facilitator has a copy of the *Family and Friends Facilitator's Guide* (item 7200-24).

Group Session 2: Recovery as a Journey

Session Goals

Group members will—
- gain a better understanding of change as a process;
- determine ways change is a choice;
- identify obstacles to change.

What to Expect

Genuine lasting change often is difficult and takes time. One of the deepest characteristics in many people's lives is the inability to delay gratification. "I want what I want, and I want it now." We need to learn to expect progress to be difficult. In relationships we often have the illusion that if one thing would change, then everything would suddenly be wonderful. "If John would just stop drinking, then I would be happy." Reality is more complicated than that. As a result, when John stops drinking and problems still exist, more, rather than fewer, difficulties arise. Group members may be resistant to this unit. Some will not want to see recovery as a journey. They want to arrive at the destination immediately.

If some group members are angry or argumentative, recognize that they may be reacting to their own situation rather than the group or your leadership. Help the members to examine their feelings about the fact that they probably will never find instant gratification. God intends for His children to develop the Christian graces including patience, gentleness, faithfulness, and self-control (Galatians 5:22-23).

Other group members may display impatience with the support-group process. Their attitude may be like the buzzard who said: "I'm tired of this patience stuff, I'm gonna go and kill something." They may complain that the support-group emphasis on identifying and dealing with feelings is a waste of time. They just want to do something. This unit can help them to see that time spent in recovery is not lazy self-indulgence but rather diligent work.

Before the Session

- ❏ Read and complete the learning activities for unit 2 in *Family and Friends* member's book.
- ❏ Confirm child-care provisions for the group if the church is providing child care.
- ❏ Make sure the room is clean and chairs are arranged in a circle with just enough to accommodate your group. Remember to leave a gap in the circle of chairs and do not place a chair in front of the door. Avoid creating a feeling of being trapped.
- ❏ Provide several boxes of tissues.
- ❏ Have tear sheets and markers available for use during the session.
- ❏ Collect enough three-by-five inch cards to allow one for each member.
- ❏ Read through the lesson plan materials and choose the sharing activities you will use with your group. Make copies of Handout 4, "Changes."
- ❏ If you choose to use the method described under the discovery-group lesson plan, invite the guest couple in advance. The guest couple should be a stable Christian couple in which one spouse has been in recovery for some life issue and in which the other spouse has experienced the struggle of adapting to the change, enlist them to come and share their journey with the group.

During the Session

Arrival—Greet the group members as they arrive for the session.

Suggested Support-Group Lesson Plan

For a support-group session, use the suggestions under day 1. Follow the instructions given. Consider using the suggestion to have a guest couple share their journey.

Suggested Discovery-Group Lesson Plan

If you know a stable Christian couple in which one spouse has been in recovery for some life issue and in which the other spouse has experienced the struggle of adapting to the change, enlist them to come and share their journey with the group. Ask the recovering spouse to share what the support group and recovery process has meant in his or her life. Ask the non-recovering spouse to share his or her struggle to relate to the support-group process and to the changes taking place in the spouse. Ask the couple to lead or participate in a time of questioning and sharing with the group.

Suggested Leadership Helps

Day 1: Change Is a Process
Call for a volunteer to read Ben's story from page 23. Explain that this week's work is about the difficulty of making lasting life change. In the following series of activities, allow members to write their responses privately then lead the group to compile a master list. By following this method you will help them to identify and own their thoughts and ideas more effectively.

Distribute three-by-five inch cards to each member of the group. Ask them to take a moment to write on one side of the card at least three lasting changes they would like to see in their friend. Allow only a few minutes for this. When they have completed their lists, brainstorm responses. Ask members to share the type of changes they have written without being overly specific or blaming the other person. Write the responses on the chalkboard or tear sheet.

Next ask members to turn their cards over and write at least three lasting changes they would like to see in their own character and behaviors. Again allow time for members to write their answers. Then brainstorm and write their responses on the chalkboard without comment other than affirmation. Feel free to affirm honest responses with statements like, "Yes, I also struggle with that problem."

Finally lead members to list reasons why change is so difficult. Include reasons why they find lasting change difficult and reasons their friend finds lasting change difficult. Seek to lead the group to include responses such as:
- because current thoughts, feelings, and actions have become habitual.
- because of deeply ingrained patterns from childhood.
- because we have learned to depend on our behaviors for protection and even if they cause us pain, we are terrified at the thought of being without them.
- because our bodies have become physically addicted to some behaviors like using caffeine or nicotine, and we fear withdrawal.

Encourage the group to name as many of the elements that discourage change as possible.

In a time of sharing, ask each member to share why change is difficult for him or her and one thing they have learned through this study to help them better relate to their friend's difficulty with change.

Day 2: Change Is a Choice
Distribute Handout 4, "Changes." Ask the members to do the first exercise on the handout. Lead members to discuss which methods are most likely to work. Ask them to describe what the likely results of each method might be. For example, to talk constantly about the changes that need to be made may make the person feel anxious, guilty, and angry. This type of approach will probably result in less positive change and more actions of the sort you would prefer to see changed. The attempts to control the other person are counterproductive. After a discussion of the approaches, ask members to share honestly which approaches they have used in the past. Be prepared to begin the sharing by disclosing an example when you have used one or more of the first three responses in the list.

Explain that while change requires a commitment, the commitment must be on the part of the person making the change, not a family member or friend. Review the summary statements for day 2 (p. 28). Ask how the statements affect our attitude toward change in our lives and in our friends' lives.

Day 3: Obstacles to Change
Distribute copies of Handout 4, "Changes" if you have not done so already. Call attention to the second activity on the handout. Allow time for members to complete the learning activity. (They should have completed the same activity in their work this week.) Lead the members to list various emotional habit patterns. Include such emotional patterns as worry, anger, and fear. The concept that emotions are habitual just as are actions may come as a surprise to some members. Lead in a time of sharing their responses to the activity.

Discuss the approach to changing attitudes from page 29. The approach involves the five parts:
- the experience,
- interpretation of the experience,
- feelings as a result of the interpretation of the experience,
- reinterpretation of the experience, and
- new feelings.

Explain that some call this process "reframing." The term refers to the fact that we look at events and situations through a frame—a point of view, like a picture frame. In the illustration in the book, Sally looked at the situation through the frame that emphasized James' thoughtless disregard for her needs. When we use the skill of reframing, we stop and ask the question, "How would this situation look to someone with a different perspective?" Review Harry's story on page 30 as an example of reframing a situation. Invite members to share an example from their lives of a situation they might need to reinterpret using the five-part method.

Day 4: Allies for Change
Share your responses to the learning activities on page 33 that ask what phrase best expresses why you find it difficult to let God help you change. Invite group members to share their responses and feelings.

Day 5: We All Change
Relate Larry Pillow's story about the stresses in his and his wife's relationships as he began recovery. If possible share how you have experienced similar stresses. Invite members to share what changes have taken place in their relationships with their friend since beginning recovery and what they are doing to adjust to those changes.

After the Session

❏ Pray for each member of the group. Pray for members with special needs.
❏ Read "Before the Session" for Group Session 3, and carefully complete all the activities in unit 3 of the member's book.
❏ Meet with your co-facilitator to review this session and to plan for Group Session 3. Pray together for your group members and any special needs they have. Pray also for yourselves.

Group Session 3: Impact of a Dysfunctional Family

Session Goals

Group members will—
- define a dysfunctional family;
- learn the rules of a dysfunctional family;
- examine the roles of dysfunctional family members;
- identify characteristics of adult children from dysfunctional families;
- gain insights about ways dysfunctional characteristics affect families.

What to Expect

Note that not all families are dysfunctional, and not all support groups deal with dysfunctional family issues. However, we are all affected by our families. You may need to help some group members understand that the emphasis on family dynamics can help all families to function in a more effective and Christ-honoring way.

You may choose to use this example. In a college curriculum students often take a course in abnormal psychology. The reason for the course is not because the students will be working with psychopaths. The primary reason to study abnormal psychology is to understand better the small amount of unhealthy behavior in every person. By studying major thought and character disorders the student can better understand the faulty thinking and the sin-damaged character in every person. In the same way, if you came from a functional family, you can still study dysfunctional families to understand how families operate.

Note that the subject matter of this unit makes for unique temptations with gossip. Help the members to understand that they are to share their own thoughts and feelings and to avoid confessing the sins of their friend. In day 1 they identified the issues that made their friend's family dysfunctional. Help members to identify the difference between understanding their friend or sharing their own thoughts and feelings—both of which are appropriate—and blaming, shaming, and gossiping about their friend's behaviors—which are inappropriate and destructive. Be careful as group facilitator that you do not lead the group to get into the latter.

Before the Session

❏ Read and complete the learning activities for unit 3 in *Family and Friends* member's book.
❏ Provide several boxes of tissues.
❏ Have tear sheets and markers available for use during the session.
❏ Read through the lesson plan materials and choose the sharing activities you will use with your group. Make necessary posters.

During the Session

Arrival—Greet the group members as they arrive for the session.

Suggested Support-Group Lesson Plan

Before the session make posters or write on several tear sheets the names of the dysfunctional family roles from day 3. Also make several small signs each with one of the rules, "Don't talk," "Don't trust," or "Don't feel." Make enough of the small signs that in the following activity each member can choose the signs they prefer.

Briefly summarize the three rules described in day 2 and the five roles described in day 3. Explain that in the dysfunctional family the members are pushed into the rigid and inappropriate roles by the rules that are at work. Also explain that these rules sometimes show up even in very functional families. Display the posters and signs as you review the concepts. Attempt to put members at ease; they can participate in the activity and sharing time without in any way suggesting that their family was dysfunctional. Explain that each person will choose from the signs the rule with which they most identify. Then they will attach their sign to the poster—thereby connecting the rule and the role. Instruct members to place their chosen sign on their chosen poster at the same time. Members will not designate which was their choice. Your goal is to create a bit of minor pandemonium. Each person will have a measure of anonymity while everyone makes their choice.

When members have returned to their seats, ask them to share both the rule and role which they chose. Don't put anyone on the spot. Encourage members to share only as much as they are willing to share.

After listening to others share, someone may need to change their choice. Perhaps they had been denying real feelings and actions but had courage to face reality after another shared. For the first time, some members may begin to identify genuinely and feel some memories and issues they have long buried.

Suggested Discovery-Group Lesson Plan

Prepare posters or signs of the dysfunctional family rules, roles, and characteristics. Say: "A great deal has been written in recent years about dysfunctional families. We want to cut through some of the hype and psychobabble and ask a practical question: 'What is a dysfunctional family and what difference does it make?'" Review with the group that this week in their personal work they have examined several different ways of looking at a family system. In day 1 they described a dysfunctional family as one in which the children do not receive appropriate nurture, guidance, and support from parents or other caregivers. In day 2 they looked at the rules—don't talk, don't trust, don't feel—that govern many families. In day 3 they looked at how families without needed nurturing skills push children into rigid and inappropriate roles. Then in days 4 and 5 they looked at characteristics of adult children from dysfunctional families.

Explain that the purpose of the dysfunctional family terminology ought never be to blame or shame. As in the case of a disease, the purpose needs to be purely to diagnose for treatment. The purpose of studying one's family of origin is not to blame or avoid responsibility. The purpose is to understand ourselves better so that we can take responsibility for ourselves in the present.

Lead the group to discuss the components that make up a functional or dysfunctional family. Ask them to work together in two's or three's to write several definitions of both a functional and a dysfunctional family. Or, if group size suggests doing so, lead the group to do this work together. If you divide into smaller groups, allow the members to report back and discuss their definitions.

If the makeup of the group and time permits, ask the group members to share at least one way in which their families of origin were functional and at least one way in which they were dysfunctional.

Suggested Leadership Helps

Day 1: Defining a Dysfunctional Family
Ask: "What do you think of when you hear the term *adult child* or *adult children*? Does the term seem negative to you? What do you think the term means?"

In the ensuing discussion, help members to identify at least two uses of the term. *Adult child* is a term that recognizes the reality of past loss. It refers to the fact that the person was not able to experience a healthy childhood. The term also recognizes the reality of present learned behavior. For me to call myself an adult child of a dysfunctional family means I recognize that I have some extra work to do to become an effective and complete person. I recognize that I have not reached the maturity in certain areas of my life that God intended.

Explain that we are not here to take our friend's inventory. In fact, we need to learn never to apply the terms *adult child* or *dysfunctional family* to another person. I can call myself an adult child, but I should never call anyone else an adult child. Be very careful in facilitating the group that you do not lead members to violate other individuals' boundaries. The skill we need to develop is to share not what others are doing so much as to share our own thoughts and feelings.

Note that the principle mentioned above is not the same as the "no-talk" rule in a dysfunctional family. The no-talk rule seeks to hide the truth. Appropriate behavior means sharing the truth with people who can be part of the solution. Gossip means sharing other people's experiences with those who are not part of the solution and for the purpose of making myself look better by making someone else look worse.

Point out that the exercise on page 40, which asks what made your friend's family dysfunctional, is to further communication and understanding. The purpose ought not be to blame, to manipulate, or to gossip. Explain that one almost universal result of living in a dysfunctional family is called *stuffing*—the learned inability to talk about or show feelings. Ask members how the inability to talk about feelings has affected their relationships with their friend or others.

Outline the three main strategies for dealing with a past dysfunctional family (p. 40).
We can—
1. Blame our present condition completely on the past.
2. Ignore the past completely.
3. Go through a process of healing to overcome effects of the past.

Ask group members to describe how they identify with Jared, Warren, or Max on page 40.

Ask the following question from page 41: "If your friend grew up in a dysfunctional family, how is the support group helping him or her deal with that reality?" Also ask: "How can you support your friend as he or she learns to deal with that reality?"

Day 2: Dysfunctional Family Rules
Briefly explain the three cardinal rules of dysfunctional families.
1. Don't talk.
2. Don't trust.
3. Don't feel.
Ask: "How were the three rules of dysfunctional families applied in your friend's family of origin? How have these three rules affected your life through your family of origin and through your relationship with your friend?"

Briefly review the three rules and the stories of Ned, Bonnie, and Allen from pages 42-43. Ask members if they can relate to any of the three rules and if so, to share a childhood memory illustrating the rule. Begin by sharing your own childhood memory experience.

Day 3: Dysfunctional Family Roles
Summarize the five roles presented in the lesson. Ask if anyone wishes to share what they experienced or learned by completing the exercises on page 45 in which they discussed the roles with their friend. How does understanding the roles affect their relationship with the friend? How does the understanding affect their feelings and thoughts about their own families?

Day 4: Dysfunctional Characteristics, Part 1
Remind members that in day four you studied the development of approval addiction. Challenge members that you are about to lead them in an exercise that will require great courage to be honest. Remind them that they are free to choose. They can choose to share or not to share. Review the exercise built upon Psalm 139:23-24 (p. 46). Lead the way by sharing your own answers. Also share how you feel when you consider your responses to the exercise.

Make a poster with the typical results of approval addiction.
- low self esteem
- choosing friends with problems
- being overly sensitive
- isolationism
- responsibility extremes

Invite members to share first how the material helped them to understand their friend and also how they relate to the five results in their own lives. Invite them to share an incident they wrote about concerning these areas (pp. 47-48).

Day 5: Dysfunctional Characteristics, Part 2
Make a poster listing the dysfunctional characteristics from day 5: denial, dependent personality, misplaced guilt, difficulty with relationships, problems follow-through problems, need to control, and impulsive behavior. Ask members to share which of the characteristics cause the greatest difficulty for their friend, and which cause the least difficulty. Then ask them to share the same responses about themselves.

After the Session

❏ Pray for each member of the group. Pray for members with special needs.
❏ Review with your co-facilitator your personal and group goals.
❏ Read "Before the Session" for Group Session 4, and carefully complete all the activities in unit 4 of the member's book.
❏ Meet with your co-facilitator to review this session and to plan for Group Session 4. Pray together for your group.

Group Session 4

Bonding and Boundaries

Session Goals

Group members will—
- determine ways bonding affects individuals;
- deal with the fact of bonding deficits;
- examine the purpose of boundaries;
- identify problems related to boundaries;
- discuss ways to overcome boundary problems.

What to Expect

You will need to remind group members of the basic premise of a *Family and Friends* group: we cannot fix or control the other person. The purpose of the group is individual growth; therefore, we will focus on ourselves. The individual work during the week gives encouragement and activities to help the group member build communication with the friend, but it would be a violation of the other person's boundaries to come to the group and tell the friend's story. The best way we can help our friends in recovery is for us to seek individual growth.

The content of this unit can easily lead to a focus on the "other person." Encourage members to see that no one is suggesting that something is wrong with them. The reason for the focus on the group member is to help us avoid the codependent behavior of trying to fix our friend.

Before the Session

❑ Read and complete the learning activities for unit 4 in *Family and Friends* member's book.
❑ Provide several boxes of tissues.
❑ Have tear sheets and markers available for use during the session.
❑ Read through the lesson plan materials and choose the sharing activities you will use with your group. Make necessary posters and copies of Handout 5, "Boundary Issues."

During the Session

Arrival—Greet the group members as they arrive for the session.

Suggested Support-Group Lesson Plan

Summarize the information on bonding from day 1. Include the information on ways we seek to compensate for lack of intimacy from the day 1 activities of FG page 38. Ask members to share ways they identify with bonding deficits. Remind them that since we are all sinners they are not being disloyal to their families by seeking to understand the family dynamics they have experienced. Ask them to share ways they have tried to deal with bonding difficulties in their lives.

After the group has shared about bonding, and if time permits, summarize the issue of boundaries from days 3 and 4. Distribute copies of Handout 5, "Boundary Issues." Ask members to share how no boundaries, unclear boundaries, blurred boundaries, or rigid boundaries have and continue to affect their relationships.

Suggested Discovery-Group Lesson Plan

Make a poster or write on a tear sheet or chalkboard the following questions: *1. What is it/are they? 2. How does it/do they develop? 3. What happens if we do not learn/develop in this area?*

Divide the group into two sub-groups. Explain that the unit deals with two basic life experiences/skills that every person needs: bonding, which results in the ability to develop and experience loving relationships; and boundaries, which make it possible to be a separate individual.

State that without healthy development in both of these areas we will have difficulty with the most important areas of life—giving and receiving love.

Ask one group to prepare a report on bonding and the other group to prepare a report on boundaries. Ask each group to answer the three questions you have displayed. Allow 10 minutes for the groups to prepare their responses.

After the groups have reported on bonding and boundaries, ask members to share their personal response to this question: "In which area of your life do you have the greatest difficulty, bonding issues or boundary issues?" Guide members as they share.

Close the meeting with the summary that we all need to grow in both of these areas. Remind members that we grow by practicing these skills. We develop bonding skills by spending time in intimate prayer with God and by building trust with others. This is one of the primary purposes of groups. We develop boundaries by practicing setting and enforcing healthy boundaries.

Suggested Leadership Helps

Day 1: Bonding Deficits
On page 54 Larry Pillow described one of the classic ways we deal with lack of intimacy: we pretend that intimacy is unimportant. Ask the group to describe as many ways as possible that people attempt to deal with lack of bonding. List and affirm their responses.

Lead them to identify at least three distinct ways we strive to compensate: we pretend that we don't need closeness; we go to the opposite extreme and cling to others—often with the result that our neediness drives them away; or we cover our need for intimacy with some compulsive or addictive behavior. Ask members to share if and how they have struggled with any of these ways of dealing with the pain caused by a lack of intimacy.

Ask members to share their responses to the activity at the bottom of page 55, the symptoms of family bonding deficits. Share your own personal reaction to the symptoms, then invite members to share.

Day 2: Dealing with Bonding Deficits
State: "The process of overcoming the effects of bonding deficits include the elements of *talking, tears, time,* and *trust.*" Ask members to describe why each of the four elements is essential. For example, talking—telling your story—is often the only way to begin to identify losses and see objectively. As long as we do not talk about our experience, we maintain our own self-induced blindness. Draw from the material in day 2 to identify the necessity of each of the four elements.

After members have described intellectually why each of the four elements are necessary, ask them to share an issue of grief with which they need to deal.

Day 3: The Purpose of Boundaries
Make a poster of the five types of boundaries from page 59: *non-existent boundaries, unclear boundaries, blurred boundaries, rigid boundaries,* and *healthy boundaries.* Summarize for the group these five types of boundaries. Ask members to describe which of the types of boundaries best describes life in their family of origin. Ask them to tell a story or give an example from their families that illustrates the chosen type of boundaries.

Ask members to share how inappropriate or unhealthy boundaries have affected their relationships.

Day 4: Problems with Boundaries
Make and distribute copies of Handout 5, "Boundary Issues," or make a poster of the chart at the top of the handout. Explain that everyone struggles to some degree with boundary problems. Ask members to describe into which window(s) on the chart they see themselves fitting.

Explain that boundary difficulties cause us either to be irresponsible or super responsible. Most of us can identify areas of our lives in which we are irresponsible and other areas in which we are super responsible. Ask members to describe in what areas they tend to be irresponsible and in what areas they tend to be super responsible.

Day 5: Overcoming Boundary Problems
Make and distribute copies of Handout 5, "Boundary Issues" if you have not already done so. Ask members to take time to review the symptoms of boundary problems and to circle those that affect their lives. Ask members to share what they have learned about themselves from this list and from the unit on bonding and boundaries.

After the Session

❑ Pray for each member of the group. Pray for members with special needs. Pray also for members who might be non-Christians. Pray for their openness to the gospel and your openness to be available for counsel.
❑ Read "Before the Session" for Group Session 5, and carefully complete all the activities in unit 5 of the member's book.
❑ Meet with your co-facilitator for review, planning, and prayer.

Group Session 5

Shame and Identity

Session Goals

Group members will—
- identify ways shame shapes a person's identity;
- compare shame and guilt;
- examine causes of shame;
- determine cures for shame.

What to Expect

Some members may be shame-bound in the extreme, and yet they may not have recognized the symptoms of shame in their lives. They may act in a number of very different ways. Some may rigidly and even angrily resist the idea that shame affects their lives. Remember that the task of a facilitator is to encourage self-awareness, but conviction is the work of the Holy Spirit. You may want to scream at some members, "Can't you see the evidence of shame in your life?" but, please, resist the temptation.

Because denial is so powerful, prepare yourself with the awareness that some members may not see the shame issue affecting their lives. But because the Holy Spirit is powerful, be patient. Some members may not respond openly, but they may be affected profoundly by the sharing in the group this week. Sometime in the future a member you thought was unaffected may share with you how profoundly the session touched him or her.

Trust the Holy Spirit, and be ready for how members of the group respond. Some may be moved deeply; they may share emotional stories of sources of shame in their lives. Others may remain intellectually stoic through the session. Pray that God will help everyone in the group more accurately to see how shame has affected their lives and relationships.

As in other sessions of *Family and Friends,* help members to see that the best thing they can do for their friend is to concentrate on understanding themselves. The suggestions in this session center not on the friend, but on the group member.

Before the Session

❏ Read and complete the learning activities for unit 5 in *Family and Friends* member's book.
❏ Provide several boxes of tissues.
❏ Have tear sheets and markers available for use during the session.
❏ Read through the lesson plan materials and choose the sharing activities you will use with your group. Make necessary posters and copies of Handout 6, "Factors that Contribute to Shame."

During the Session

Arrival—Greet the group members as they arrive for the session.

Suggested Support-Group Lesson Plan

Use either the day 2, day 3, or day 4 suggestions for the basis of sharing. Guide the group to share feelings rather than intellectual content. If members give only cognitive responses, ask them to relate a situation in which they felt shame. Ask them to tell how they *feel* rather than simply to tell what they think or to describe what happened.

Suggested Discovery-Group Lesson Plan

Divide the group into two work groups. Assign group one to describe causes of shame. They may use the material in days 3 and 4. Assign group two to describe practical actions we can take to deal with and dispose of shame.

Allow the groups to work for 10 minutes, then call for reports. On a tear sheet or chalkboard list the causes of shame in one column and the cures for shame in another column. After the group has cognitively discussed the issue, ask members to share their personal feelings related to the issue of shame. Refer to the lists. Ask: "With what causes of shame have you struggled? What actions are you taking to overcome shame messages in your life?"

Day 1: How Shame Shapes Identity
Ask members to describe their sources of positive identity as a child and as a youth. The question appears on page 67, but do not encourage members to read the answer they have written. Encourage them to share their thoughts and feelings at the time of the meeting.

Day 2: Shame and Guilt
Ask members to brainstorm the difference between guilt and shame. On a chalkboard or tear sheets write the words *guilt* and *shame*. Beneath each word write all of the words or phrases the group members suggest. Lead the group to clarify that shame is about who we are while guilt is about what we do. Guilt may or may not be legitimate, but since shame attaches to our personhood, it cannot be judged objectively. Ask members to think of and share two events—one in which they did something wrong and felt guilt and one in which they had done nothing wrong and felt shame.

Day 3: Causes of Shame, Part 1
Brainstorm attitudes or events in a person's family of origin that can be a source of shame. List the group's responses. After they have responded compare this list to one on page 70. Explain that just as we absorb shame from other people, we can choose to "give them back their shame." Ask members to think of a time when they have felt shame. The incident can relate to one of the family of origin issues in the brainstorming exercise, or it can be some other event. Ask members to share the incident and to share how they might choose to give back the shame. Encourage members that they may make the declaration that they are giving back the shame right there in the group. Affirm the responses of the group members.

Day 4: Causes of Shame, Part 2
Make and distribute copies of Handout 6, "Factors that Contribute to Shame." Ask members to take a couple of minutes to respond to the activities on the handout. After they have completed the handout, lead the group in sharing factors that have contributed to a feeling of shame in their lives.

Day 5: Cures for Shame
Make a poster with the following information.
1. God's grace to pardon, forgive, and cleanse our guilt and shame.
2. Learning to share our feelings of shame with trustworthy and supportive people.
3. Learning to accept ourselves unconditionally as God accepts us.

Lead the group in a time of brainstorming answers to the question, "How can we get rid of our feelings of shame?" Record the group's answers on a chalkboard or tear sheet. Affirm their responses. Be certain that the answers include the ways of dealing with shame highlighted on the poster.

After the Session

❑ Pray for each member of the group. Pray for members with special needs.
❑ Read "Before the Session" for Group Session 6, and carefully complete all the activities in unit 6 of the member's book.
❑ Meet with your co-facilitator for review, planning, and prayer.

Group Session 6: Looking to the Future

Session Goals

Group members will—
- recall what they have learned about support groups and dysfunctional families;
- review specific issues that affect their relationship with their friend;
- review the nature of change and evaluate their progress as well as that of their friend;
- determine changes they plan to make;
- survey options for additional study.

What to Expect

If you are following the six-week format, this will be your final session. You will need to give attention to bringing closure to the group. Closure means helping members "tie up their emotional loose ends concerning the group experience." Some members may have just begun to feel comfortable and safe in the group. The end of the group sessions will represent an emotional loss to everyone, but these group members may feel the loss more acutely.

You may want to reserve time at the end of the session to ask how group members feel about the group coming to an end. Encourage members to identify and express their feelings. You may make plans for follow-up fellowship activities. Encourage the members to make plans to continue their personal growth after the end of the group.

If you are continuing with the three optional units, you will encounter the same grief and loss at the end of unit 9. When you make plans for the final group session, refer back to this unit. Remember to help your group members to achieve closure.

Before the Session

❑ Read and complete the learning activities for unit 6 in *Family and Friends* member's book.
❑ Provide several boxes of tissues.
❑ Have tear sheets and markers available for use during the session.
❑ Read through the lesson plan materials and choose the sharing activities you will use with your group. Make copies of Handout 7, "Review Questions."

During the Session

Arrival—Greet the group members as they arrive for the session.

Suggested Support-Group Lesson Plan

Copy and distribute Handout 7, "Review Questions." Explain that far more review questions are provided than they can answer in one meeting. Ask members to share their response to one area that has been particularly important in their lives. Guide the sharing. Affirm the growth you see in the members. Encourage them to consider continuing their growth journey. If you will be continuing with the three optional units, encourage members to prepare for the next session. If this will be your final session, guide the group as members process their feelings and possibly make plans for any follow-up group or future group reunion.

Suggested Discovery-Group Lesson Plan

Ask members to brainstorm the concepts, understanding, or areas of growth they have experienced in the six weeks of the group. Ask each member to share the one area in which he or she has grown most and the one area in which he or she most desires to grow. Review the suggestions for further study in day 5. If you will be continuing with the three optional units, encourage members to prepare for the next session. If this will be your final session, guide the group as members process their feelings and possibly make plans for any follow-up group or future group reunion.

Suggested Leadership Helps

Day 1: Evaluating Your Experiences
Review the story of Keri (p. 79). Ask members to share

what they think might be the outcomes of her attempts to avoid being like her parents. Review the activities for possible answers. Ask members to describe how a Christ-centered support group might help Keri. Brainstorm as many answers as possible. Write all the suggested answers on a chalkboard or tear sheet. Do not evaluate any of the answers, affirm the members who suggest possibilities. Next ask members to describe how the support-group experience has helped them or their families. Members may draw from the responses you wrote in the previous activity.

Day 2: Reviewing Specific Issues
Ask the following questions to review the progress members have made since beginning the group.
1. How has an understanding of support-group life helped you better understand your friend?
2. In what ways has your experience in this group been similar to that of your friend?
3. If your friend grew up in a dysfunctional family, how has a knowledge of these rules helped you understand the way he or she relates to you?
4. What progress have you and your friend made in overcoming the effects of dysfunctional family rules?
5. What do you and your friend need to do to continue making progress?
6. Do you or your friend identify with any of the roles of a dysfunctional family? If so, which ones? How have these roles affected your relationship with your friend?
7. Which of the dysfunctional family characteristics do you identify in your friend? Which do you identify in your own life?

Day 3: Examining the Process of Change
Ask members to share based on the following questions.
1. In what ways do you see your friend continuing to look for quick and simple solutions? In what way do you see yourself seeking a quick-fix rather than being able to delay gratification?
2. What is the most difficult challenge for you in relating to the process of changes in your friend's life? Are changes taking place too slowly, too quickly, or too radically?
3. What is one positive change you have made in the way you relate to your friend?

Day 4: Identifying Choices and Changes
Invite members to respond to the following review questions.
1. What insights have you gained during this study about processing emotions? What changes have you made in the way you process your emotions because of these new insights? What other changes would you like to make in the way you process your emotions?
2. Through your work and sharing in this support group, what new insights have you gained into God's grace?
3. How would you like to change in the way you respond to God? How would you like to change in the way you respond to your friend?

Day 5: Additional Options for Study
Ask members to share their responses to the following activity they completed in day 5. Invite them to share their plans for how they can grow in one of the areas they have chosen as priorities. Encourage members to recognize that a small but consistent change is better than attempting more than they can deal with. Encourage them to choose one area on which to concentrate their efforts at growth.

✎ **Think about areas in your life in which you need to grow. Check your top three priorities from the following list.**
❑ Understanding the Bible.
❑ Changing unhealthy relationships.
❑ Dealing with issues related to family of origin.
❑ Developing your prayer life.
❑ Building self-esteem.
❑ Knowing God's will.
❑ Caring for your physical needs.
❑ Building witnessing skills.
❑ Becoming a disciple maker.

After the Session

❑ Pray for each member of the group. Pray for members with special needs.
❑ Review with your co-facilitator your personal and group goals.
❑ If you will be continuing the group, read "Before the Session" for Group Session 7, and carefully complete all the activities in unit 7 of the member's book.
❑ Meet with your co-facilitator. If you will be continuing with the three optional units, review this session and make plans for Group Session 7.

If this has been the last session, review with your co-facilitator the entire six weeks of study and sharing. Pray for the group members as they continue to process their feelings without the benefit of the group sessions.

Group Session 7: Anger

Session Goals

Group members will—
- gain a better understanding of anger;
- identify myths about anger;
- develop skills in processing anger;
- determine ways to prevent inappropriate expressions of anger;
- learn to forgive those who offend.

What to Expect

Some members may respond to this unit with great enthusiasm. They may realize for the first time that they have lived by the false belief embodied in the myths about anger which are recorded in day 1. Others may be deeply in denial about the existence or legitimacy of anger.

Be aware that people who cannot process their anger appropriately often transfer that anger and direct it against some other target. Prepare yourself for the possibility that these members may be critical of the unit, of the group, and of your leadership. You may, and hopefully will, detect some expressions of anger from your group members.

If you are the object of a member's anger, recognize that the material is hitting too close to home. Do not take displaced anger personally. Calmly guide the members to respect one another's boundaries as they share and process their feelings.

Some members may attempt to deal with this topic entirely from an intellectual standpoint. Gently help them to identify their feelings. Ask them to share what they are feeling rather than simply what they think. Direct their attention to the feelings chart and ask them to identify what they are feeling. You may need to help such a member to identify the fact that he or she is denying feelings. You sometimes may need to ask: "John, may I just be a mirror for you? You have said what you *think* about the episode you shared, but you have not shared what you *feel* about the event."

As you model sharing on this issue, demonstrate honesty and trust to group members. You model these characteristics by showing your own flaws and failures. As you share one or more examples from your own life of dealing with anger, beware of sounding like the "person who has it all together." Do not share only stories of your success. Make the choice to share times when you have failed to deal in the best possible way with anger. By sharing your failure you will communicate two things to members. You will show that you trust the group enough to be honest. You also will demonstrate that you are genuine and trustworthy.

Before the Session

❑ Read and complete the learning activities for unit 7 in *Family and Friends* member's book.
❑ Provide several boxes of tissues.
❑ Have tear sheets and markers available for use during the session.
❑ Read through the lesson plan materials and choose the sharing activities you will use with your group. Make necessary posters and copies of Handout 8, "Anger."

During the Session

Arrival—Greet the group members as they arrive for the session.

Suggested Support-Group Lesson Plan

Display a poster containing the six steps to learning to forgive from day 5. Also make and distribute copies of Handout 8, "Anger." Explain that every person on earth must deal with anger. Anger is part of being human. When we pretend that we never have to deal with anger, we become dishonest with our emotions and our anger comes out sideways.

Ask members to share what they find most difficult about dealing with anger. Suggest that they may draw from all the work they did this week as well as from the handout and poster. Begin the sharing by telling what you find most difficult about dealing with anger.

After members have shared, if time permits, review the steps on the poster and ask: "What truth or principle in the material have they studied this week has been most helpful in learning to deal with anger?"

Suggested Discovery-Group Lesson Plan

Make and distribute copies of Handout 8, "Anger." Divide the group into sub-groups of two or three or allow them to do this individually. Assign each sub-group one of the myths about anger. Ask the sub-groups each to prepare a report explaining why one of the myths about anger is false and unbiblical.

Allow them a few minutes to prepare their reports. Affirm the work that the individuals or sub-groups have done. Then assign the same groups the principles of anger and ask them to share how they have personally experienced the assigned principle. Some groups or individuals may have more than one principle. Allow members to share.

Briefly review the material on root causes of anger from day three. Ask members to share the root cause of anger with which they most identify. If time permits ask them to share an episode from their experience of anger that illustrates the root cause.

Suggested Leadership Helps

Day 1: Myths and Principles of Anger
Distribute copies of Handout 8, "Anger." Ask the group members to review the list and to share their answer to two questions.
1. What principle or myth about anger was most enlightening or helped you most in understanding anger?
2. What are some ways of expressing anger that you have learned?

Ask members to share what myth and/or principle about anger was most present in their childhood homes. Next ask members to share their method(s) of dealing with anger.

Day 2: Problems Caused by Anger
Ask members to share their method(s) of dealing with anger. Ask: "What are some choices you can make to deal with anger more effectively?"

Outline the five areas in which pent up anger causes us harm: *physical, mental, emotional, relational,* and *spiritual.*

Ask members to share examples of times when pent up anger has caused them difficulty.

Day 3: Processing Anger
Describe an experience from your own life when you have experienced and then processed your anger. Share how you—
• recognized that you were angry;
• identified the root cause of your anger;
• chose to process the anger in a constructive way.
Or, you may choose to share an example of a time when you processed your anger in a destructive or passive-aggressive manner. Invite members to think of a recent situation in which they experienced anger. Ask them to share the positive and the negative aspects of how they processed the experience.

Day 4: Preventing Unhealthy Anger
Ask members to react to the opening paragraph of the lesson: "Preventing all anger is not an appropriate goal. Preventing unhealthy or inappropriate ways of processing anger is an appropriate goal. One action we can take to help prevent inappropriate expressions of anger is to take definite steps to develop a healthy self-awareness."

Divide the group into sub-groups of two or three. Ask members to describe an occasion in which they experienced anger. Ask them to talk through with their partners their responses to the four questions on page 97.
• What am I trying to gain?
• What am I trying not to lose?
• What am I really reacting to?
• What am I trying to change?

On a poster list the five principles from the lesson for preventing unhealthy anger.
• Develop a healthy self-awareness.
• Maintain a balanced life.
• Accept what cannot be changed.
• Avoid anger-producing situations.
• Learn to forgive.
Lead the group to discuss the principles and to describe ways that they may apply them to their lives.

Day 5: Learning to Forgive
Make a poster listing the steps to learning to replace anger with forgiveness.
  Step 1: Name the offender.
  Step 2: Acknowledge your anger.
  Step 3: Describe the offense.
  Step 4: Give up the right to get even.
  Step 5: Change feelings about the person.
  Step 6: Offer forgiveness.

Summarize to the group the information from day 5 on forgiveness. Share an occasion from your life when you have worked through anger. Share how each of the steps above applied to your processing of anger. Ask members to share where they are in processing some specific area of anger in their lives.

After the Session

❑ Pray for each member of the group. Pray for members with special needs.
❑ Read "Before the Session" for Group Session 8, and carefully complete all the activities in unit 8 of the member's book.
❑ Meet with your co-facilitator to review this group session, plan for Group Session 8, and to pray for group members. Be sure to pray for yourselves as you lead.

Group Session 8

Addiction

Session Goals

Group members will—
- define addiction;
- learn characteristics of addiction;
- identify contributing factors to addiction;
- examine strategies for living with addicts;
- gain an understanding of the difficulties in overcoming addiction.

What to Expect

Just as all support groups do not deal with dysfunctional family issues, not all support groups deal with addictive behaviors. Be prepared to help members understand that even if their life situation does not involve addiction, they can learn from this unit. By studying this unit they can grow in their ability to relate to and minister to others, especially their friend in recovery.

Since addiction is such a shame-inducing issue, be prepared for some members to react defensively to the topic. Some members may talk openly about their own addictive behavior or that of a friend. Others may refuse to talk or may even become offended. Those who have learned the "no talk" rule may consider this session with hostility. By this time you know your group. Do not push members to make admissions or see truth for which they are not ready. Invite everyone to study the topic objectively, but also build in time for personal sharing.

Since some members may have experienced deep hurt as a result of an addict's behavior, be prepared for possible anger and blaming. Gently help members to see that their feelings are to be acknowledged. Help them to see that a group can be a safe place to express those feelings. At the same time, encourage them to move beyond bitterness and blaming. You can draw upon what members have studied in the earlier units to help them see that the forgiveness process begins with acknowledging the full reality of an offense, continues with grieving that offense, and only then, after processing the thoughts, feelings, and behaviors related to the event, can a person genuinely forgive. For an additional resource on this process see *Search for Significance LIFE® Support Group Series Edition*, pages 176-180.

Before the Session

- ❏ Read and complete the learning activities for unit 8 in *Family and Friends* member's book.
- ❏ Provide several boxes of tissues.
- ❏ Have tear sheets and markers available for use during the session.
- ❏ Read through the lesson plan materials and choose the sharing activities you will use with your group. Make copies of Handout 9, "Addiction."

During the Session

Arrival—Greet the group members as they arrive for the session.

Suggested Support-Group Lesson Plan

Read the following paragraph taken from "Stages in Development of Addiction" (p. 106).

> Addiction begins with an internal change. This change is seen in the resources persons turn to for emotional and spiritual support and growth. Normally, persons turn to family and friends, God, self, and the larger community for love, nurture, and support. If individuals do not develop relationships within these four groups, they turn to other types of relationships. This is where addiction comes in.

Now read together and discuss the essay "Addiction and Relationships" in Handout 9.

Lead members to discuss briefly the essay on relationships. Discuss how it feels to be "the loneliest person in town" or to be a friend or spouse to "the loneliest person in town." State that the person married to an addict may be the only person lonelier than the addict. Guide members as they share their feelings about relationships and addiction.

Suggested Discovery-Group Lesson Plan

Distribute copies of Handout 10, "If I were an addiction...." Divide the group into sub-groups of two or three persons each. Give the groups the following assignment.

> An addiction is like a living thing, and anything that is alive will fight to stay alive. Draw from everything you know and what you have learned in this unit this week. Your assignment is this: if you were an addiction of any kind, to a substance or to a behavior, describe how you would fight to stay in control of your host.
>
> You will have 10 minutes to list every possible means you—the addiction—would use to make your host come back to you and repeat the addictive behavior.
>
> If you run out of ideas, you may answer a second question: "If you are like a living thing, what caused you to exist in the first place?"

Ask a third question if time permits: "What do people mean when they describe you (addiction) as cunning, baffling, and powerful"?

After 10 minutes, call for reports. List and affirm answers members give. Seek to help them to include the following answers. "If I were an addiction I would use...
1. physical withdrawal symptoms. I would attempt to make the person so nervous, uncomfortable, or even life-threateningly ill that she would repeat the addiction.
2. pain killing effect of using. Whenever the addict performs the behavior, I would relieve both emotional and physical pain, thus making the addict want to return.
3. low self-worth. I would make the addict feel that he is not worth the effort to change.
4. advertising through all the media.
5. peer pressure.
6. stress in relationships thus making the addict desire a means of escape.
7. guilt. I would seek to cause the addict to get into a cycle of acting out followed by guilt and shame followed by more acting out to ease the pain of guilt.

If time permits, allow the groups to process the second question: "If you are like a living thing, what caused you to exist in the first place?" Discuss the material in day 3 of the member's book to determine the answers. Help members to include in their discussion each of the following factors that contribute to the development of an addiction.
1. Genetics
2. Family of origin
3. Personal choices

As time permits discuss the first portion of day 2 to describe the meaning of cunning, baffling, and powerful.

Conclude the session by asking: "What did you learn this week that helps you better understand the recovery task faced by addicts?"

Suggested Leadership Helps

Day 1: Defining Addiction
Ask members to brainstorm thoughts about addiction. Encourage them to include definitions of addiction, fragments of definitions of addiction, and descriptions of addiction. Record their responses on a chalkboard or tear sheets. Help them to include such elements as:
- to control mood
- substance or behavior
- develop greater tolerance
- need more of the substance or activity
- withdrawal when deprived of the addictive agent
- cunning, baffling, and powerful

Ask members to share their definition of addiction. Affirm members' responses though some may be inadequate. Review the summary statements on page 105.

Day 2: Characteristics of Addiction
Lead the members to discuss ways addictions are cunning, baffling, and powerful (p. 105). Record their responses.

Ask, "Is expecting an addict to change his or her behavior reasonable? Why or why not?" Help members to see that the question demands both a definite positive and a definite negative response. Yes, the addict must take responsibility. One slogan in AA reads: "Only you can do it, but you can't do it alone." The statement reflects both responses. Only the addict can make the changes in his or her life. On the other hand, no, the addict cannot change the behavior alone. He or she needs the power of God and the support of healthy people to overcome addiction. One person in a group said: "Addictions are like living things, and anything that is alive will fight to stay alive."

Help members to see that those who deal with addictions must avoid two extremes. They must avoid simply blaming the addict and saying, "He could stop if he wanted to." Addictions are powerful. The addict cannot simply "stop if he wanted to." On the other hand, members must avoid the opposite extreme. They must not say, "Oh, the poor addict is so sick, she just can't help herself." The truth includes elements of both sides. The addict needs help, but the addict must do the work.

Day 3: Causes of Addiction
Ask members to describe factors that contribute to addictions. Lead them to include and discuss each of the following factors.
1. Genetics. Some of us seem to be more susceptible to certain addictions than others. Thus for example, if a person has a family history of chemical dependency, that person is at a greater risk of becoming a chemical dependent, should he or she ever use chemicals.
2. Family of origin. The behaviors and ways of coping with problems that we learn from our families either increase or decrease our likelihood of developing addictions. If a child learns healthy, effective, and Christ-honoring ways of solving problems, that child will be less likely to develop an addictive behavior. If the child does not learn to cope effectively with life, he or she will be more likely to turn to and become attached to some destructive substance or behavior.
3. Personal choices. While our genetics and family of origin may increase our susceptibility to a destructive life pattern, our choices are what lead us into that pattern.

Day 4: Breaking an Addiction
Describe both Margaret's and Bob's stories from pages 110-111. Ask members why they think Margaret's recovery seems to be so much more successful than Bob's. Discuss the fact that while both Margaret and Bob were church members and apparently both Christians, Margaret experienced spiritual and emotional growth through discipleship and support groups. Say: "Old timers in many recovery groups say that one factor most often makes the difference between those who find lasting life change and those who do not. That one factor is a genuine relationship with God."

Point out that in the story of Bob's struggle with addiction, he "even talked about helping others by starting a recovery ministry." Many times people who have not developed a deep and lasting discipleship rush out prematurely to "save the world." Explain that the inability to delay gratification—the inability to wait for future fulfillment—is a primary characteristic that leads to addiction and that describes the addictive personality. For example, if a person was reared in a family in which a parent did not keep promises or was unreliable, the child learns to get what he or she can immediately. The child does not develop the skill of waiting for or working toward a future reward. Ask members to share if and how they struggle with the inability to plan for the future, to stick to a task until completion, or to wait for a future reward.

Explain that one reason *MasterLife* discipleship training has been successful in prison relates to this issue. Many of us did not learn the skill of delaying gratification. Growth as a disciple through *MasterLife* helps the students to develop those life skills. Whatever life problem we are facing, we can always benefit by concentrating on our walk with the Lord. In fact, often the only way to solve a given problem is to leave the problem with Jesus, get out of the way, and get busy growing as a disciple. While we are busy, the Lord solves the problem.

Day 5: Dealing with Addiction
Lead the group to discuss the section of the member's book entitled "Admitting a Need" (p. 112). Ask: "Why is it true that we cannot make the decision to seek help for the addict?" In the ensuing discussion, help members to see the difference between efforts to control the addict's behavior—that result in greater irresponsibility—and efforts to help the addict face reality.

If you have group members whose friend is an active addict, you can help greatly by assisting the members to understand the difference between attempting to make the person stop—which seldom helps—and the process called *intervention*. In an intervention a person who cares about an addict does several things.
1. The person enlists competent, usually professional, help.
2. Together the person and the professional helper determine who can have an impact on the addict. Those people might be employers, family members, friends, coaches, or teachers.
3. The person who cares for the addict enlists the helpers and together they prepare to confront the addict.
4. Before confronting the addict, the interveners make arrangements for treatment options so that if the addict agrees to enter a residential treatment program, one is available immediately. They also prepare to answer the objections the addict will make.
5. Then by confronting the addict at the best possible time and place, they greatly enhance their chances of success. Only the addict can make the choice to admit reality and seek help, but through intervention those who care can increase the likelihood of that positive outcome.

After the Session

❑ Pray for each member of the group. Pray for members with special needs.
❑ Read "Before the Session" for Group Session 9, and carefully complete all the activities in unit 9 of the member's book.
❑ Meet with your co-facilitator to review this group session and to plan for the next group session. Remember as you plan that Group Session 9 will be the last session. Pray for the members as they try to put a closure on this study and for yourselves as you lead the group.

Group Session 9

Depression

Session Goals

Group members will—
- gain a better understanding of depression;
- examine the causes of depression;
- identify consequences of depression;
- learn ways to prevent and overcome depression.

What to Expect

Since this unit deals with depression, be aware of several possible reactions. You may have one or more seriously depressed persons in your group. The group setting may be the first opportunity in their lives that they identify what they are experiencing as depression. In some cases the very discovery that a person is suffering from depression may seem to aggravate the situation. Be prepared to recommend qualified Christian counseling if someone in the group needs care. Both for reasons of liability and because the person needs to make his or her own decisions, always recommend more than one counselor and allow the person to choose.

An almost opposite possibility can also result. Some persons can begin to find signs of depression where few or none exist. They can use the topic as an escape from reality rather than a step toward positive action. Seek to keep the group meeting focused in a positive direction. The emphasis needs to be on how one can deal with depression rather than encouraging members only to identify the problem.

Before the Session

- ❏ Read and complete the learning activities for unit 9 in *Family and Friends* member's book.
- ❏ Provide several boxes of tissues.
- ❏ Collect enough three-by-five inch cards for each member to have one.
- ❏ Have tear sheets and markers available for use during the session.
- ❏ Read through the lesson plan materials and choose the sharing activities you will use with your group. Make necessary posters.

During the Session

Arrival—Greet the group members as they arrive for the session.

Suggested Support-Group Lesson Plan

Prepare two posters before the session. On the first poster write the 12 symptoms of depression (from day 1). On the second poster write the 12 ways to deal with depression (from day 5). Briefly review the lists and the material about depression. Advise the group that in this session they will want to share briefly because they will have two opportunities to do so. First the group will share on the topic, "How I relate to the symptoms of depression." After each person has had an opportunity to share on the first topic, ask members to share from the second list, "The best way I have found—or a way I might use—to prevent or deal with depression."

After a time of sharing, bring the group to a close. Express your feelings for the group. Encourage members to make plans for continued growth. You might plan a follow-up fellowship to celebrate the completion of the group.

Close the group with a circle of prayer. Ask members to express their feelings to God about the group and their fellow members.

Suggested Discovery-Group Lesson Plan

Prepare two posters before the session. On the first poster write the 12 symptoms of depression (from day 1). On the second poster write the 12 ways to deal with depression (from day 5).

Divide the group into two sub-groups. Ask one group to prepare a five-minute report on the symptoms of depression. Ask the second group to prepare a five-minute report on the methods of dealing with depression. Explain that each report will be followed by a time of discussion and sharing. Assure them that their report can be as simple as a review of the lists. Allow them 10 minutes to prepare their reports. Then ask them to present the reports. Following each report, lead the group in sharing how the topics relate to their lives.

Ask each member to share the most important thing he has learned about himself during this study.

Encourage members to continue their growth after the conclusion of this group. Direct them to the suggestions at the end of unit 6 on pages 85-87. Make any plans for a follow-up fellowship or reunion.

Close the session and the group with a time of prayer. Suggest that members express to God their gratitude for whatever growth they have experienced during this group.

Suggested Leadership Helps

Day 1: Symptoms of Depression
Make a poster of the 12 symptoms of depression from the first lesson (listed below), or write the symptoms on a chalkboard or tear sheet.

1. Withdrawal
2. Extreme self-criticism
3. Self-preoccupation
4. Passive attitude
5. A negative outlook
6. Loss of interest in life
7. Resentment of happy people
8. Radical change in eating habits
9. Chronic fatigue
10. Hypochondria
11. Increased use of alcohol or drugs
12. Hopelessness

Ask members to describe a time when they or their friend was experiencing depression. Ask them to share which of the symptoms they most experienced and how they felt. Ask them to describe how they have coped with or recovered from the depression. If they do not identify with the symptoms of depression, ask them to share from the friend's point of view.

Ask members to share what Scripture passage has been most helpful to them when they have been depressed. What Scripture has been most helpful to their friend when he or she has been depressed?

Day 2: Causes of Depression
Distribute three-by-five inch cards to the group members. Summarize the five causes of depression (from pp. 118-120). List the five causes on a chalkboard or tear sheet. Ask each member to write the five causes on their card and to rank them in the order that they affect the member's life. Assure them that the card is for their eyes only. Members may ask questions or briefly discuss the five causes. After members have made their lists, ask those who wish to share to describe how one or more of the symptoms has affected or is affecting their lives.

Day 3: Consequences of Depression
Briefly summarize the consequences of depression outlined in day 3. Ask members to share their responses to these two questions from page 122.
1. How does it make you feel about the depression of your friend (or your own depression) to know that many biblical characters have struggled with depression?
2. What spiritual consequences do you notice in your life or in the life of your friend (or your own life) as a result of depression?

Encourage members to answer the questions verbally. If they struggle to answer, you may want to direct them to the answers they wrote during the week.

Day 4: Overcoming Depression, Part 1
State that the temporary and ineffective cures people seek are all methods of medicating our depression. The problem is that the methods make the depression worse by adding additional problems such as health difficulties, debt, guilt, and relationship problems. List the five ineffective cures described in day 4.
1. Overeating
2. Shopping
3. Inappropriate affection
4. Busyness
5. Alcohol and other drugs

Ask members to share briefly if and how they struggle with these behaviors. Affirm the members as they answer.

Day 5: Overcoming Depression, Part 2
Display a poster or tear sheet with the following list of ways to deal with or prevent depression.
1. Exercise
2. Sharing
3. Good eating habits
4. Medicine
5. Music
6. Hobbies

7. Serving others
8. Keeping a journal
9. Humor
10. Bible study
11. Reading
12. Prayer

Ask members to share three things regarding the list.
1. What methods have you used in the past to prevent or deal with depression?
2. What are you doing now?
3. What is one thing you might consider doing to improve your life in this area?

After the Session

❑ Meet with your co-facilitator. Review the entire nine weeks of study and sharing. Also review your personal and group goals. Pray together for each group member.
❑ Call members and encourage them to follow through on their plans for continued growth.

Handout 1 — My Identity

As a way to begin to get to know one another, we will do the following exercise. The exercise is intended to be fun and to give you the structure to share parts of your personal history. We develop intimacy by sharing details of our lives in appropriate and safe ways. You will have an opportunity to share the following five things. You may choose to share only those elements of your identity that you trust your group members with.

My name:
My functional identity:
My personal identity:
My secret identity:
I am here because _____

My functional identity is what I do—wife, mother, electrician, etc. My functional identity involves no intimacy.

My personal identity is who I am as a person apart from my tasks. I am a Christian, a person who cares about certain art and music, etc. Personal identity involves a greater degree of intimacy.

My secret identity can be that person others don't know because they don't take time to listen to me. It may be my hidden hopes, dreams, fears, or shame. "I am an aspiring writer, airplane pilot, poet. I am a person who fears being known or found out. I am a person who seems confident but who often feels lonely and afraid."

§ You have permission to reproduce this page for use with your *Family and Friends* group.

Handout 2 — Our Relationship-Recovery Story

When one member of a couple or other relationship is in recovery, both people in the relationship are affected. Therefore the story of how the relationship has changed and is changing is a part of your recovery story. As a part of this group meeting you will share a portion of your relationship-recovery story. Do not be intimidated. You may share as little of your story as you feel comfortable with. Your facilitator will begin the process by sharing an example of a relationship-recovery story.

As you share, seek to follow these guidelines.

1. To practice good boundaries, do not tell about your friend or family member's behaviors or recovery; instead, share your own journey. In other words, do not blame or confess your friend's sins. In groups this is called "not taking someone else's inventory." Read the following examples.

Right: "Hi, my name is John. I am here because my wife is in recovery. I have experienced difficulty understanding and relating to the changes going on in her life. I feel left out, angry, and afraid."

Wrong: "Hi, my name is John. I am here because my wife is in a _____ group. She is doing all these crazy things. She is angry. She won't fix my dinner and she never cleans the house anymore."

2. Do not divulge confidential information such as names of people in a group, things your friend has done, or the identity of your friend or family member's sponsor.

3. You have the right to your own boundaries. You do not have to share anything which you are not comfortable sharing. You may simply say:

"Hi, my name is _____. I am here because I have a friend who has been in recovery. I have felt _____ from this _____ with the process and I hope to gain _____ group."

The above guidelines are not intended to limit your sharing in this meeting. They are intended to help you to feel safe. You may share as much of your recovery relationship story as you desire within the time limitations of the group.

§ You have permission to reproduce this page for use with your *Family and Friends* group.

53

Handout 3   Levels of Sharing

Level 1:
Engaging in small talk, such as "How was your day? How are you feeling?" This involves sharing information but not sharing deep feelings.

Level 2:
Sharing facts about people and events.

Level 3:
Sharing ideas and opinions.

Level 4:
Open and honest communication. Sharing feelings of the heart, as well as the head.

Handout 4   Changes

✎ What approach do you think would be the most effective way to encourage your friend to make necessary changes? Select from the list.

- ☐ Constantly talk about changes that need to be made.
- ☐ Discuss changes that need to be made in front of friends.
- ☐ Every day tell your friend how much it means for him or her to make the necessary changes.
- ☐ Earnestly pray for your friend.
- ☐ Encourage your friend to continue in the support group.
- ☐ Other: _____

✎ Why are emotional habit patterns difficult to break? First, check those that apply to you. Then write an x beside those that apply to your friend.

- ☐ I won't admit they exist.
- ☐ I don't realize they are harmful.
- ☐ I lack objectivity.
- ☐ I expect others to adjust to my behavior.
- ☐ My actions get the desired results.
- ☐ I compare myself with others who have worse habits.
- ☐ My emotional outbursts "just happen."
- ☐ It takes too much work to change.

Handout 6

Factors that Contribute to Shame

In the unit you answered the following exercises relating to your friend's recovery. Please complete them again in relation to your feelings of shame.

✎ In what ways has culture contributed to your shame? Circle those things that contribute most to your feelings of shame. Add items to the list that apply to your shame.

- overweight
- not a good athlete
- failure in career
- other _____
- not good looking by society's standards
- mediocre in career
- not in good physical shape

✎ Check responses or behavior choices you have made that created additional shame. Add others not on the list.

☐ destructive behavior
☐ violent outbursts
☐ other: _____
☐ self-pity
☐ withdrawal

✎ Is perfectionism a problem for you? If so, in what way is it apparent? Check the items that apply to you.

☐ frequent failure to complete a project
☐ procrastination
☐ making too much of insignificant details
☐ self-esteem based on performance
☐ competitive with and critical of others
☐ makes excuses for quality of work
☐ demands perfection of others

✎ Complete the following statements.

To me shame feels like _____

I feel shame when _____

§ You have permission to reproduce this page for use with your *Family and Friends* group.

55

Handout 5

Boundary Issues

Four Categories of Boundary Problems

	CAN'T SAY	CAN'T HEAR
"No"	Feels guilty and/or controlled by others	Wants others to take responsibility for him
"Yes"	Self-absorbed; doesn't respond to other's needs	Can't receive caring from others

Symptoms of Boundary Problems

- extreme feelings of obligation
- hidden anger and resentment toward demands of others
- inability to be direct and honest
- excessive people-pleasing
- life out of control
- no sense of identity as to "who I am"
- inability to fulfill work demands
- tendency to blame others or circumstances for mistakes
- excusing or denying failure
- chronic depression
- chronic anxiety
- compulsive behavior (eating, substance abuse, sex, money)
- chronic relationship conflicts

§ You have permission to reproduce this page for use with your *Family and Friends* group.

Handout 7 — Review Questions

1. How has an understanding of support-group life helped you better understand your friend?
2. If your friend grew up in a dysfunctional family, how has a knowledge of these rules helped you understand the way he or she relates to you?
3. What do you and your friend need to do to continue making progress?
4. Do you or your friend identify with any of the roles of a dysfunctional family? If so, which ones? How have these roles affected your relationship with your friend?
5. Which of the dysfunctional family characteristics do you identify in your friend? Which do you identify in your own life?
6. In what ways do you see your friend continuing to look for quick and simple solutions? In what way do you see yourself seeking a quick-fix rather than being able to delay gratification?
7. What is the most difficult challenge for you in relating to the process of change in your friend's life? Are changes taking place too slowly, too quickly, or too radically?
8. What is one positive change you have made in the way you relate to your friend?
9. What insights have you gained during this study about processing emotions? What changes have you made in the way you process your emotions because of these new insights? What other changes would you like to make in the way you process your emotions?
10. Through your work and sharing in this support group, what new insights have you gained into the grace of God?
11. How would you like to change in the way you respond to God? How would you like to change in the way you respond to your friend?

§ You have permission to reproduce this page for use with your *Family and Friends* group.

Handout 8 — Anger

Myths about Anger

Myth 1: The absence of anger is desirable, even the ideal.
Myth 2: All anger is destructive.
Myth 3: Anger is the root cause of the actions of angry people.
Myth 4: Anger is always an unchristian response.

Principles of Anger

Principle 1: Anger is universal.
Principle 2: The method of expressing anger is a learned behavior.
Principle 3: Anger is energy.
Principle 4: Anger is often synonymous with pain.
Principle 5: Anger is not a sin.
Principle 6: Anger is a secondary emotion.

§ You have permission to reproduce this page for use with your *Family and Friends* group.

Handout 8   Addiction

Addiction and Relationships

Addiction can be approached from several different viewpoints, each of which has some truth. Addiction can be described as a habit, a repetitive behavior. It includes an element of pain relief, both physical and psychological pain. Addiction certainly has something to do with family-of-origin issues. But we want to look at addiction from another standpoint: it is an attempt to get our relationship needs met. God intended that we would each turn to family and friends, to community, and to Him to get our needs met. To turn outward to others requires certain skills. Many people do not learn those skills. Instead addicts practice what some call "nurturing through avoidance." Addicts try to get their relationship needs met by turning inside. All addictions have this in common: the real action is taking place inside the addict. The addict is seeking to change his or her own internal mood. This turning away from relationships is why being an addict or being in a relationship with an addict is the "loneliest job in town." In A.A., they say, "addicts don't have relationships, they take hostages." This is also why recovery must be about relationships. Recovery is the process of learning to have relationships.

§ You have permission to reproduce this page for use with your *Family and Friends* group.

Handout 9   "If I were an addiction..."

Instructions:

"An addiction is like a living thing, and anything that is alive will fight to stay alive." Draw from everything you know and what you have learned in this unit this week. Your assignment is this: if you were an addiction of any kind, to a substance or to a behavior, how would you fight to stay in control of your host? List every possible means you—the addiction—would use to make your host have to come back to you and repeat the addictive behavior.

If you are like a living thing, what caused you to exist in the first place?

Describe what people mean when they describe you (addiction) as cunning, baffling, and powerful.

§ You have permission to reproduce this page for use with your *Family and Friends* group.

57

Sample Letter to Participants in Support Groups

Dear Friend of Support-group Ministry,

As you probably know, few experiences in life can result in such basic change in a person as does participation in a support group. Many of us have experienced significant change and growth through the support-group ministry. Often we hear someone say: "Second only to becoming a Christian, this is the greatest thing that has happened in my life."

You may also be aware that change always creates tension in relationships. Many times when a person begins the recovery process the spouse or friends have difficulty relating to the changes in their loved one. The result can sometimes be broken relationships or even broken marriages.

A basic maxim of recovery is that "It gets worse before it gets better." When friends see the recovering person dealing with deep grief, they naturally worry that recovery is hurting rather than helping. As a result, they often fight against rather than cooperate with the changes in the loved one. In some cases the non-recovering spouse or friend feels afraid, left out, alienated, or jealous of the emotional intimacy experienced in the group. As a result of these natural and normal fears, recovery can stress or even destroy relationships.

We are seeking to provide help for family members and friends of persons in recovery by offering a group called *Family and Friends: Helping the Person You Care About in Recovery*. The group will help family members or friends better understand why those of us in recovery experience changes. The group will discuss the importance of issues such as shame, identity, and a dysfunctional family. Group members will work on ways to improve communication and also will examine themselves for their own recovery issues. Some of them may choose to begin their own recovery journey.

I would like to invite family members or friends of those people who have been or are involved in our support-group ministry. But therein lies the problem. We have not, nor will we violate your confidentiality. So I am writing to ask if you know family members or friends that you would like to see participate in a *Family and Friends* group. If you do, consider the following possibilities.

1. Give me names, addresses, and phone numbers of those persons, in which case I will contact them, and state: "Your friend _____ suggested that you might be interested in participating in our *Family and Friends* group.

2. If you would prefer that I not contact them, please talk to me and I will supply you with more information about the group so that you may talk with them.

Please call me if you have questions. My number is: _____.

Yours in Christ,

Sample Letter to Prospective Participants (Support-Group Format)

Dear _____,

Support-group ministry has made an impact in many lives. However, you may have noticed a possible downside. When one member of a family or relationship begins the recovery process, that change often creates problems for his or her family members or friends. Sometimes the changes can strain relationships to the point of threatening friendships or marriages. Sometimes recovering individuals overreact and go to extremes in their new-found recovery.

I am pleased to announce that we will be offering a group called *Family and Friends: Helping the Person You Care About in Recovery*. This study is for family members or friends of someone who is in recovery. It will help participants to understand what support groups do—and what they do not do. Participants in *Family and Friends* will learn to understand better why those in recovery experience the changes they do. The group will discuss the importance of issues such as shame, identity, and a dysfunctional family. Group members will work on ways to improve communication with their recovering friend or family member.

I want to invite family members or friends of those who have been involved in our support-group ministry to consider being involved in a *Family and Friends: Helping the Person You Care About in Recovery* group. If you would like to learn more about recovery or about the *Family and Friends* group, I will be having an informational meeting to answer such questions at:

Date: _____

Time: _____

Place: _____

Or, you may call me if you have questions. My number is: _____.

Participating in a *Family and Friends* group can be an enriching and growing experience for you, and it can be the best thing you could do for your friend who is in recovery.

Yours in Christ,

Sample Letter to Prospective Participants (Discovery-Group Format)

Dear _____,

Support groups have proved to be a powerful means of discipleship and personal growth. Many people have deep needs that can be ministered to through support groups. But you may have asked such questions as: "What really happens in a support group? How does someone get involved? Is this process biblical? What about trained leaders?"

As a means to help church members and leaders understand support-group ministry and to develop potential leaders, our church is offering a course called *Family and Friends: Helping the Person You Care About in Recovery*. *Family and Friends* is written to help persons who have never been in a Christ-centered support group to learn about the groups.

You may have wondered why people participate in support groups, or you may have considered whether God would have you to minister through support groups. This group provides an opportunity for Christians to learn about support groups in a non-threatening way. Participants in a *Family and Friends* group will consider such topics as:

    Support Group Life
    Recovery as a Journey
    Impact of a Dysfunctional Family
    Bonding and Boundaries
    Shame and Identity
    Looking to the Future
    Anger
    Addiction
    Depression

I would like to invite you to consider participating in a *Family and Friends* group. If you would like to learn more about recovery or about the *Family and Friends* group, we will be having an informational meeting to answer such questions at:

Date: _____

Time: _____

Place: _____

Or, you may call me if you have questions. My number is: _____.

Yours in Christ,

Feelings Poster

Anger

Fear

Joy

Guilt

Sadness

LONELINESS

Shame

Other?

Promotion Ideas

In addition to the sample letters to send to prospective participants (pp. 58-60), use these ideas for posters, bulletin inserts, and your church's newsletter.

For support-group format

Family & Friends

A support group for those with family members or friends of someone who is in recovery.

Informational meeting is _____
at _____ in room _____.

For questions, call _____.

Text is *Family and Friends: Helping the Personal You Care About in Recovery.*

For discovery-group format

Family & Friends

A discovery group for those want to understand support-group ministry.

Informational meeting is _____
at _____ in room _____.

For questions, call _____.

Text is *Family and Friends: Helping the Personal You Care About in Recovery.*

Family and Friends: Helping the Person You Care About in Recovery

Our church is offering a support group for family members and friends of someone who is in recovery. Participants will learn:

- what support groups do and do not do
- to understand better why those in recovery experience the changes they do
- the importance of issues such as shame, identity, and a dysfunctional family
- ways to improve communication with their recovery family member or friend

The group will begin on _____.
For more information, contact _____.

Family and Friends: Helping the Person You Care About in Recovery

Our church is offering a course called *Family and Friends: Helping the Person You Care About in Recovery*. This group provides an opportunity for Christians to learn about support groups in a non-threatening way. Participants will consider such topics as:

- Support Group Life
- Recovery as a Journey
- Impact of a Dysfunctional Family
- Bonding and Boundaries
- Shame and Identity
- Anger, Addiction, Depression

The group will begin on _____.
For more information, contact _____.

The Church Study Course

The Church Study Course is a Southern Baptist education system designed to support the training efforts of local churches. It provides courses, recognition, record keeping and regular reports for some 20,000 participating churches.

The Church Study Course is characterized by short courses ranging from 2½ to 10 hours in length. They may be studied individually or in groups. With more than 600 courses in 24 subject areas, it offers 200 diploma plans in all areas of church leadership and Christian growth. Diplomas represent hours of study, knowledge and skills acquired, and approval of the sponsoring agency.

While the heart of the Church Study Course is leadership training, many courses are available for all members. Each year, approximately 800,000 awards and 150,000 diplomas are earned by adults and youth. While youth may receive credit on any of the courses, some courses are designed especially for youth. Also available in the system are non-credit short courses for children and preschoolers.

Originating in 1902 with two Sunday School courses, the Church Study Course now serves all church programs and is jointly sponsored by many agencies within the Southern Baptist Convention. Sponsors include: Baptist Sunday School Board, Woman's Missionary Union, Brotherhood Commission, Home Mission Board, Foreign Mission Board, Stewardship Commission, Education Commission, and the respective departments of the state conventions and associations affiliated with the Southern Baptist Convention.

Records are kept by the Sunday School Board for the other agencies. A state-of-the-art computer system maintains records for more than 1,500,000 individual students from 106 countries. Regular reports are provided to participating churches. After enrollment in a diploma plan(s), diplomas are issued automatically as requirements are met. Credit earned in one church is recognized in all other Southern Baptist churches.

Complete details about the Church Study Course system, courses available, and diplomas offered may be found in a current copy of the *Church Study Course Catalog*.

How to Request Credit for this Course

This book is the text for course number 17-233 in the subject area: The Christian Family/Counseling—Study and Teaching. This course is designed for five hours of group study.

Credit for this course may be obtained in two ways:

1. Read the book and attend class sessions. (If you are absent from one or more sessions, complete the "Personal Learning Activities" for the material missed.)

2. Read the book and complete the "Personal Learning Activities." (Written work should be submitted to an appropriate church leader.)

A request for credit may be made on Form 725 "Church Study Course Enrollment/Credit Request" and sent to the Awards Office, Sunday School Board, 127 Ninth Avenue, North, Nashville, Tennessee 37234. The form on this page may be used to request credit. Enrollment in a diploma plan may also be made on Form 725.

DUPLICATE AS NEEDED

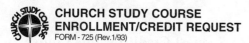

CHURCH STUDY COURSE ENROLLMENT/CREDIT REQUEST
FORM - 725 (Rev.1/93)

MAIL THIS REQUEST TO ▶ CHURCH STUDY COURSE RESOURCES SECTION
BAPTIST SUNDAY SCHOOL BOARD
127 NINTH AVENUE, NORTH
NASHVILLE, TENNESSEE 37234

Is this the first course taken since 1983?   ☐ **YES** If yes, or not sure complete all of Section 1.   ☐ **No** If no, complete only bold boxes in Section 1.

SECTION 1 - STUDENT I.D.

Social Security Number

Personal CSC Number*

☐ Mr ☐ Miss
☐ Mrs.

DATE OF BIRTH ▶ Month Day Year

STUDENT
Name (First, MI, Last)
Street, Route, or P.O.Box
City, State | Zip Code

CHURCH
Church Name
Mailing Address
City, State | Zip Code

SECTION 2 CHANGE REQUEST ONLY (Current Inf. in Section 1)

☐ Former Name
☐ Former Address | Zip Code
☐ Former Church | Zip Code

SECTION 3 - COURSE CREDIT REQUEST

Course No.	Title (Use exact title)
1. 17-233	*Family and Friends: Helping the Person You Care About in Recovery*
2.	
3.	
4.	
5.	
6.	

SECTION 4 - DIPLOMA/CERTIFICATE ENROLLMENT

Enter exact diploma/certificate title from current Church Study Course catalog. Indicate age group/or area if appropriate. Do not enroll again with each course. When all requirements have been met, the diploma/certificate will be mailed to your church. Enrollment in Christian Development Diplomas is automatic. No charge will be made for enrollment or diplomas/certificates.

Title of Diploma/Certificate	Age group or area
Title of Diploma/Certificate	Age group or area
Signature of Pastor, Teacher, or Other Church Leader	Date

*CSC # not required for new students. Others please give CSC # when using SS # for the first time. Then, only one ID # is required. SS# and date of birth requested but not required.